"This book provides answers and action for women who are caught in the insidious cycle of psychological, emotional and physical abuse in their relationship. Congratulations to Michelle Hollomon for tackling this important issue that gets little attention in Christian circles, but happens inside some Christian homes more than we like to admit. Michelle offers a practical approach to helping women reclaim their lives, heal past wounds, and make a better future for them and their children."

—Danielle Madrid,
Founder and Executive Director of
Havens Community Connections,
a nonprofit that helps women build exit
strategies out of the domestic abuse cycle.

"Reading this book will forever change how you think about yourself and your relationships. Women who read this book will feel as though they are talking to a friend who really gets it. They will be able to identify what kind of relationship they are in, how they got there, and how to find strength and hope for their future. Every day, I see the how broken and abusive relationships affect women and their childreN. This book changes lives one relationship at a time."

—Jennifer Paddock, MDIV, Executive Director AOD,
program serving homeless women and children
recovering from domestic violence and addiction.

"With advice that is both practical and profound, Michelle Hollomon shows how to find healing from past wounds and tackle relationships problems for good. Every reader will emerge from this book with a

greater sense of self, empowerment and hope. I look forward to using this book in my practice and to gift to my friends."

—Genevieve Rideout MA, LMHC

"Michelle brilliantly exposes the charade of users and abusers, and how they causes people to lose out on real love. This is a thought-provoking and powerful must-read. As a psychotherapist, I am shocked at how society gives narcissistic and abusive behavior a pass. The consequences of unchecked and unbridled narcissism is taking a toll on the health of our culture, children and families. Michelle provides the expertise and tools to end these consequences and to see your relationships more truthfully. Explore this book to be empowered, gain confidence, increase your respect and ultimately gain freedom."

—Joanna Flemons, MS, LCSW

"Do you have an unhealthy knack for entering unhealthy relationships? With the same grace and skill as in her first book, therapist Michelle Hollomon, MA, LMHC, skillfully offers an understanding of why you are drawn to toxic people. Her wisdom evokes thought for anyone who finds themselves entangled with what she cleverly calls "losers, users and abusers." Read this to learn more about yourself, your relational patterns, and how to learn to recognize and avoid entanglements with harmful people. Begin the life-changing process of choosing relationships with greater intentionality with this insightful book. This work includes exercises to recognize and disentangle yourself from unhealthy people."

—Cherrie Herrin-Michehl, MA, LMHC

Losers, Users, and Abusers
and the Women Who Love Them

How to Break Free from Destructive

Relationships and Get the Love You Want

Michelle Hollomon, LMHC
Licensed Mental Health Counselor

Losers, Users, and Abusers and the Women Who Love Them: How to Break Free from Destructive Relationships and Get the Love You Want

Copyright © 2018 by Michelle Hollomon
ISBN: 978-0-692-95429-4

This is Dedicated to Sweet and Sassy,
and to your future Mr. Dashings.

Contents

Acknowledgements

Without the support of my family and friends, a project like this would not be possible. Mr. Dashing, your belief in me and in this project helped me keep the faith, stoke the fire, and find the time. Thank you to the women in my circle who stand their sacred ground every day. I'm so lucky and blessed to be a part of your lives. Thank you to the Fabulous Five—you are walking this journey out and inspiring the next generation who follows you. Plus, you're all really foxy. Thank you to the Mamas of the Bible who can laugh, cuss, cry, and hallelujah all in the same breath. Thank you to the faithful leaders at Northwest Christian Writers Association who consistently encourage the writer with a dream.

Introduction

I was fooled. I believed what he said. He cast and I bit, hook, line, and sinker. He had the PhD, the convincing pedigree, and reputable people vouching for him. He had the charm, the promises, the plan. Sure, there were some red flags, but nothing I couldn't handle. Or so I thought.

After the investment of time, reputation, and money, to my shock and personal horror, I discovered I had been misled. Taken. Used. And lied to.

How did a smart gal like me fall for a Shmo like him? I had just written my first book, and I desperately wanted it to do well. Publishing people had taken a risk on me, and I wanted to "prove" to them they hadn't made a mistake. It was that desperation that made me vulnerable, made me believe things that were too good to be true. My false need to prove my worth made me susceptible to empty promises.

What blind spots did I have that prevented me from seeing through his shiny veneer?

What patterns can be observed in exploitative relationships? Can victims of exploitation be rescued, healed, and returned to wholeness?

These were the questions I asked myself. Luckily, I had supportive counselors, friends, and family in my life who helped me recover from this professional injury. My career, finances, and ego had been badly bruised, but the wonderful people who love me held my heart. My husband, Mr. Dashing, who is probably the most supportive man on the planet, reminded me that money, jobs, and opportunities come and go, but relationships are what really matter. Thankfully, this event did not damage my relationships.

I began to think about those women who are *married* to the Shmo. What about the User? Or the Abuser? What about the women who don't just experience loss professionally or financially like I did, but are joined at the heart to the Abuser, suffering all levels of loss—loss of security, loss of personal safety, loss of self-respect, loss of hope, and loss of love?

What about the women who sacrifice ALL to keep their marriage and family together, even if it means they lose themselves in the process?

Not many months after my Bamboozlement by Shmo, I sat down at my dining room table and considered all I knew about the Loser, the User, and the Abuser personalities, and the women who love them. For the first time in my professional career, I was awakened to the exploitative nature in some relationships. Sure, I had counseled women in domestic violence situations before, and knew how destructive some relationships could be, but now I understood personally how manipulation and dishonest motives can lead to exploitation and abuse in relationships. I recognized my own blind spots and "soul holes." I saw for the first time how the Users in my childhood had groomed me for future exploitation as an adult. Like a puzzle coming together, piece by piece, I could see the strategies and tactics that they used to trick, groom, and fool me, and to ultimately, but unsuccessfully, try to own me.

That dining room table was littered with ideas and research findings, examples, and stories. I knew at that moment that I had tapped into something groundbreaking. Those ideas became the following facts:

Fact #1: Every person needs the Vital Three: To be Seen, Known, and Accepted Unconditionally.

Fact #2: If the Vital Three needs are not met, Soul-Holes grow.

Fact #3: Soul-Holes attract Losers, Users, and Abusers who intensify worthlessness and loneliness.

Fact #4: Soul-Holes heal by being Seen, Known, and Accepted Unconditionally.

Fact #5: Healing Soul-Holes starts with you.

Those facts became the book. The book will become your life line, your recovery, and your pathway back to wholeness.

I know that my ordeal could have been much worse. It is my personal belief that God protected me and used these events in my life to awaken me and give me new purpose. Not only has my passion increased for victims of such exploitation, but my counseling practice has flooded with women who experience all manner of psychological, emotional, or spiritual maltreatment in their relationships. There are women everywhere who feel hopeless about their relationship problems and powerless to fix them. They put on a brave face at work, bunco, and school drop offs, but feel completely alone and unloved in their marriage. The marriage advice from the pulpit and marriage books may be helpful for marriages dealing with *typical* problems like finances, parenting, and communication, but these women don't face *typical* relationship problems. These women face problems at home that are far worse than "typical."

Many women in exploitative relationships are further imprisoned by mythologies within the Christian church. Sometimes the church has a hard time believing that abuse happens inside its membership. It can be soft when addressing abusive or manipulative treatment in marriages. Often, the marriage is seen as more valuable than the individuals it represents. The view of the husband as the spiritual leader and the wife as the submissive helper can create an environment in which power imbalances are the norm, and inequality is acceptable. The Christian church can be so afraid of divorce that it turns a blind eye to the narcissistic exploitation of power and the manipulative emotional abuse that occurs in some of its marriages.

. . . .

Sometimes the church has a hard time believing that abuse happens inside its membership.

. . . .

The advice these women are given is short-sighted, useless as a Band-Aid on a heart attack. They hear advice like pray for him, have sex with him, talk to him, forgive him, pray together, go on dates together, try harder, show more respect, give it to God, and give it some time. On their own, none of these solutions work, because they deny the root of the problem.

Women are dangerously advised to be more supportive, more loving, more understanding, more submissive, more respectful, or more sexual. They are led to believe if they just try harder, their husband will finally be pleased with them enough to love them.

Typical solutions won't work for these relationships because these relationships are far from typical. Loser, User, and Abuser relationships operate under a system of power imbalances, control mechanisms, and smoke and mirrors. The rules are ever-changing, as the shiny veneer slowly cracks and the marriage is more dead inside than alive. Where a typical marriage may respond positively to marriage retreats or advice books, a Loser, User, or Abuser relationship will become even more entrenched in harmful patterns, showing no measurable sign of improvement. Interventions that don't address the psychological, financial, emotional, physical, and sexual exploitation and abuse within the marriage will only further harm the partner being abused.

· ·

Typical solutions won't work for these relationships because these relationships are far from typical.

· ·

Women who feel alone and beaten down in their marriage are susceptible to this bad advice. They themselves are in denial about how abusive their relationships really are. They need names to call the things they are experiencing, affirmation that they are not crazy, and concrete tools to change the situation.

If you are reading this book, it is likely that you are willing to work hard and make sacrifices, if only you had a plan that actually worked, a plan that didn't tell you to "overlook the bad" and "focus on the good." A plan that works won't excuse or justify bad behavior in the name of "Christian forgiveness," or incite abuse of power with antiquated hierarchical family structures.

How bad is it?

The reality is that one in four women will experience domestic violence at some point in her life. Without help, girls who witness domestic violence are more vulnerable to abuse as teens and adults, and boys who witness domestic violence are far more likely to become adult abusers of their partners and children.

Every year, of the women who are victims of homicide, one in three is murdered by her current or former partner. Psychological abuse, such as threatening rage, name-calling, emotional manipulation, and hostile intimidation is just as damaging as physical abuse, and occurs more than we know because psychological abuse is under-reported.

The good news is that you are not as powerless as you may feel. When you are awakened, you become the person with the most leverage to change your situation. A woman motivated by truth and love has unparalleled power to shape her relationships, change her happiness trajectory, and impact the next generation for good—if only she has access to the right plan.

In this book, I will not only reveal the root cause of these cold and harmful relationships, I will also walk you through the steps toward healing and wholeness. Together, we will tackle the big and small problems in your relationships. I'll shine a light on that dark place that keeps you hooked in harmful patterns, and empower you to make true changes for yourself, your relationship, and the next generation.

. . . .

Families are only as strong as the women
who take care of them.

. . . .

Breaking free from psychological manipulation and physical abuse is not only possible, it is imperative for the health of your family and culture at large. Families are only as strong as the women who take care of them. Empowering women to find their God-given value and break free from the grip of relationship abuse produces life and freedom for generations. Your family. My family. Your kids and their kids. We have the power to break harmful patterns, to be happy again, and to change the future forever. Thank you for joining me on this journey. It will be life changing.

Introduction

A Word About the Contents of this Book

About the Genders: Although both genders can be abusive to their partners, I've written this book for women as my primary audience. For the purposes of this book, I have addressed the unique similarities between women who attract partners who mistreat them.

About the Stories: The examples used in this book are illustrative in nature only. Although the stories are based on true events, they do not contain any identifying details, professions, locations, or names. Relationship themes and dynamics were kept the same, while all details were changed.

About Faith: I've written this book to be as inclusive as possible, while still staying true to my own beliefs. In my desire to be relentlessly helpful, I want this book to be as accessible as possible to each reader, regardless of religious background or faith system. I know that most readers will be in significant pain when they choose to pick up this book, and in need of practical solutions. If I did not believe that asking God for help was a part of the practical solution, I would not add it. Reestablishing your spiritual relationship to God through prayer, journaling, and meditation gives you a sense of identity, connection, and worth. Through research and experience, I have discovered that prayer and the support of loving people who pray are paramount in the healing journey. Though some of my readers will not share my Christian faith, I think they will find the book applicable and adaptable to their relationships and beliefs.

Chapter 1

Getting the Love You Want

"In our life there is a single colour, as on an artist's palette, which provides the meaning of life and art. It is the colour of love."
—*Marc Chagall*

Married to a Loser

She didn't want a divorce. In fact, she wanted to grow old with him, but she couldn't see herself living like two roommates for the sake of the kids forever. It wasn't like they fought a lot, and it wasn't like either of them had done something unforgivable, it was just that they didn't share anything anymore. She tried to reach out to him. She tried to talk about things that were interesting to him, but he emotionally stiff-armed her.

Beth and Carl seemed like they had so much going for them. They had good jobs, twin daughters and a house in a good neighborhood. Why did they feel so distant? So cold? Why did he pull away? He'd say, "Nothing is wrong, Beth. Why do you have to make everything a big deal?"

"But I feel like you're a million miles away, Carl. Why won't you just talk to me?" Sometimes Carl would respond with defensiveness.

He would yell, they would fight, and for a little while, even though it was the same old fight that was never resolved, Beth felt that closeness she craved. Fighting was better than silence. Other times, when Beth longed for affirmation and intimacy, Carl stonewalled her with his silence. She felt like the marriage was too fragile to handle going deeper. She intuitively knew that forcing him deeper would reveal the nothingness that was there.

Sometimes Carl would stay late at work and be too tired to talk. Beth wondered if Carl was depressed, or having an affair, or if something was seriously wrong with her and she had unrealistic expectations of marriage. Beth instigated fights with Carl just to get a reaction from him so she wouldn't have to feel a nagging loneliness. She wondered if there was anything worse than feeling all alone in a marriage.

Beth was married to a Loser. Carl was losing out on truly knowing Beth. The emotional intimacy she craved was the very thing he was too afraid to give.

In Love with a User

"It's like the betrayal is happening all over again. Every time my kids meet one of his new girlfriends, my heart breaks. It penetrates like the first time." My friend and I walked our dogs down the river's edge trail as rain misted our faces. "I know he has every right to date who he wants to date, and it's none of my business, but I swear, when I call and I hear a woman's voice in the background, it still hurts."

Ed and Teresa had been amicably divorced for 4 years and had recently started talking more often as they helped plan their daughter's graduation. Ed had two affairs while he was married to Teresa, and eventually he moved out to be with someone else. Through cold puffs of air, Teresa described Ed as a good and decent man who had a few problems—a guy with a messed up childhood who really wanted to be a good husband and father but couldn't quite get his act together.

"Michelle, we even started talking reconciliation recently. We were working so well together on the graduation party plans, it kind of felt like old times. We were really connecting. He was coming to church more often, pitching in on the graduation prep, giving me compliments—you know, showing all the signs. Then, last week, when I called to get some info, he was evasive, and I heard a woman's voice in the background. Why? Why did I fall for it again?!"

Ed knew how to work all the angles, prime all the pumps, and keep all his options open. When Teresa first discovered Ed's infidelity years ago, she remembered feeling completely dumbfounded. She couldn't identify any warning signs. For the entirety of their marriage, she had suspended reality. Because he seemed too good to be true, she just stopped questioning. She wanted to believe the dream more than she wanted to be aware of the truth.

Teresa loved a User. She saw the good in him when no one else could. She believed the best in him even when he stopped believing in himself. She stood up for him, even when he didn't deserve it. He gravitated toward her when he didn't have anyone else, and because she loved him, she didn't resist. Even after all those years, and all those affairs, and the way his addictions affected her kids, she still wanted to be there for him, hoping that he would finally love her the way she loved him.

Near the end of our walk, I asked, "What are you going to do now? Now that you know he is with someone else?"

Teresa smiled sadly, "I'll pull away and try to not fall for it again."

Escaping an Abuser

April never saw it coming. Not this. Not her. As she tapped on the notification from her bank, she saw that her bank account had been almost totally wiped out.

"A withdrawal? But I didn't make a withdrawal." April had a sick feeling in the pit of her stomach as she called the bank.

The teller responded evenly, "There was an electronic transfer of $10,000 to the account of a Seth…" April's hands went clammy and she hung up the phone without saying goodbye. She sat down to keep her knees from buckling. She knew Seth would not pick up his phone. Plus, it made him angry when she called him at work. Why didn't he tell her he was going to make such a big withdrawal? He must have a good reason for going behind her back and withdrawing her money. But without telling her first? Why had she given him access to her bank account in the first place?

It had all started five months ago. April was a 29-year-old interior designer. She loved her work, but the income was inconsistent and unpredictable. She'd been single a while now, and although she hated to admit it, sometimes she wished a man would take care of her so she wouldn't feel so desperate all the time.

She had seen Seth several times at church. Seth was devilishly handsome, successful, and oh so arrogant. She could barely stand him, the way he talked about himself all the time. Until he turned his attention toward her…

Once they started dating, he pushed her to do things she didn't really want to do. Her world got smaller and she became more and more dependent on him, as if he could provide everything she needed. Isn't that what she wanted after all—someone to take care of her?

April's best friend didn't like Seth, but she just didn't see him the way April saw him. April could look past the bravado and the possessiveness, and see the hurt puppy inside. Yes, there were times that he was rough and controlling, but that was because he loved her so much, right? She hoped that if she just loved him the way he needed to be loved, he wouldn't have to be so rough and controlling. He just needed to be loved the right way.

Seth wanted her to move in with him, but she wanted to wait until after he proposed. That's when her bank notified her of the big withdrawal. Seth put a down payment on a house with the money, and they would move in together by the end of the month.

On move-in day, April disagreed with Seth about where the couch should go and instructed the movers differently than Seth. To her horror, he took her to the master bedroom closet, hit her hard in the stomach, and then pinned her to the closed door. Towering above her, he breathed, "Don't ever disagree with me in front of other people again."

This was only the beginning. There would be more abuse—financial, sexual, physical, and psychological. April was love-trapped by an Abuser, and it would take an Act of God, the kindness of strangers, and levelheaded determination to get her free again.

The Statistics

An estimated 1 in 4 women will be victims of domestic violence at some point in their lives. Nearly 1 in 5 teenage girls who have been in a relationship said a boyfriend threatened violence or self-harm when presented with a break up.[1] Almost 1 in 4 women who visit an ER for injuries are abused by someone they love. Every day in the US, more than 3 women are murdered by their husbands or boyfriends.[2]

---

1   http://domesticviolencestatistics.org/domestic-violence-statistics/

2   Bureau of Justice, Bureau of Justice Statistics, *Homicide Trends from 1976-1999,* (2001).

These are the statistics we can measure, but there is so much more abuse than what is reported. Psychological manipulation, gaslighting,[3] threatening intimidation, and domestic financial exploitation are all examples of abuse that is rarely reported. If physical or psychological abuse is not happening to you, chances are it is happening to someone you know.

Your Story

It doesn't matter if your relationship is hot or cold, sweet or sour; loving, losing, using or abusing, you no doubt want more authentic love. You know what I mean—the real stuff. You want the kind of love you can feel, the kind of love that has actions and evidence and devotion to prove it. You want to feel valued, important, understood, and secure. You want the energy you put into loving your partner to last and to mean something. You want something better for you, and for your kids. You want to learn how to love and be loved *better*.

In this book, you'll learn about the Vital 3 and how they can heal Loser, User, and Abuser relationships. You will be empowered to see yourself as a valuable and worthwhile person, know yourself with deeper understanding, and love yourself with God's unconditional love. You will learn how to heal old wounds, fill old holes, to see your partner differently, and to connect in a new way.

---

3 *Gaslighting* means to manipulate (someone) by psychological means into questioning their own sanity. Source: Dictionary.com

Chapter 2

What Your Heart Already Knows

"A man travels the world over in search of what he needs. And he returns home to find it."

—*George A. Moore*

Fact #1: It's not Love without the Vital Three: To be Seen, Known, and Accepted Unconditionally

Fact #2: If the Vital Three are not met, Soul Holes grow.

Fact #3: Soul Holes attract Losers, Users, and Abusers that intensify feeling unloved.

Fact #4: Soul Holes fill by being Seen, Known, and Accepted Unconditionally.

Fact #5: The Vital Three start with You.

This book will show you how.

This book helps women experience the Vital Three in their relationships with God, with themselves, and ultimately with others, so they will no longer attract or be attracted to Losers, Users, or Abusers. If you are already in a relationship, you will learn ways to communicate with your partner that change the atmosphere of the relationship. You will learn how to invite him to join you in healthier relational habits. Whether he chooses to join you is out of your control, but you can be confident and secure about your choices leading to healthy relational living.

As a mental health counselor, I've spent thousands of hours with people problem solving, thought changing, and heart healing. I work with shy children, old couples, divorced people, people who should be divorced, stay-at-home moms, helicopter parents, single-minded corporate executives, parents of prodigals, and anxiety-ridden college students. Different folks walk through my office doors for different reasons, but all of them have one thing in common: their relationships are just plain hard to manage.

I can relate. The relationships in my life are the things that can bring me to my knees, crush me to pieces, blindside me and almost, yes, *almost* break me. It's in the context of these relationships that I grow, re-invent, re-create, humble myself, fall, fail, get up again, try, and then fly. So it is for all of us. If we learn how to navigate the complex relationships in our lives, they have the potential to heal us, grow us, and make us into truly happy people.

My nine-year-old daughter's school choir resurrected a Depeche Mode song with the lyrics, "People are people so why should it be, you and I should get along so awfully?" When she came home singing these lyrics, we both looked at each other quizzically. Good question, right? The lyrics demand an answer, yet this forty-year-old mother struggled to find the words to explain it when she asked, "What does it mean?"

I said what any good therapist/mother would say, "What do *you* think it means?" That bought me a little time.

She said, "Um, that people are sometimes mean to each other?"

"Yeah," I said. "Sometimes people are."

"But why? Why are they mean?"

"Because they didn't have amazing mothers like *you* have." And then we laughed out loud for a long time because it's both true and absurd at the same time. True because I know I'm a good enough mother, but absurd because no mother can be good enough to produce a perfectly un-mean person. Even nice people hurt each other.

That's because there's a thing called sin.

"Sin shmin," you may say. I understand. The word *sin* can conjure up hell, fire, and brimstone sermons or be relegated as outdated terminology that has lost its meaning in our postmodern culture. So, let's give sin a spin.

Sin is a crime against love.[4]

An aim and a miss.

A wrong forcing out right.

Sin is falling short of the call to love people as you love yourself, to treat others the way you'd want to be treated, to make *anything* more ultimate than Love. Love is sacrificing for the good of someone else, and it not feeling like a sacrifice because you love so much. Love is feeling welcome and safe and respected all at once. Love is doing the hard thing when everyone else is doing the easy one.

God *is* that Love. Love comes from God, and it's because of God that we have any kind of Love at all. But because we are prone to sin, we fall short of the whole-hearted Love we were created to give and receive. Instead of choosing true Love, we choose more expedient, more glamorous, more tantalizing ways to get our love-fix. These false-love ways make us feel empty, used, and alone.

---

4   *Merriam-Webster's Collegiate Dictionary.* Eleventh ed., s.v. "sin."

We intend, plan, and wish for Love, but we sin it away just the same. We sin on ourselves, and we sin on each other, and we ultimately sin against Love. It's the essence of being human.

If we're not careful, we will sin love away completely.

The Dance Floor We are Born On

My husband took some friends and me dancing for my fortieth birthday. Any '80s Material Girl will tell you that a party begins with the pre-party in the bathroom. Loud music, hot irons, nail polish, and ten already-tried-on fashion fails cluttering the floor. Everything must be. Just. Right. Once I picked the dress, I called for backup confirmation from the babysitter and my preteen daughters. Does this go together? Is this dress too tight? I swear it fit last year. Is it okay to wear these orthotics? No? Okay. Do I look, you know, old? Are pantyhose in or out? I never know! What about my eye makeup? I'm going for smoky, does it look smoky? Hey, watch me do the Running Man. Dab. Look! I still got it!

Groan. "Mom, go—you're gonna be late!"

That night, we danced till my knees hurt, and then we danced some more.

Relationships are like that dance. We anticipate, we prepare, we get advice, and then we dance. We pick our partner with hopes of reeling and laughing and closeness and love, and for a while, the dance is great. But as time goes on, and life's demands increase, the dance gets harder. The steps become more complicated. More skill is required to maneuver the steps. We end up stepping all over each other's toes with territorial ego and unchecked insecurities. We spin to the music, all the while afraid our partner won't catch us. We discover that other dance partners look better, stronger, safer. We compete and blame, and act a tough game. The dance floor becomes a boxing ring where we throw jabs and then limp back to our corners. If the dance becomes too much of a struggle, we may leave the dance floor altogether. Some of us think, "Maybe I was never meant for dancing in the first place," or "If I were a better dancer, my partner would love me," or "If he were a better dancer, this would work."

Sin looks like a really messed up dance, with deafening noise and fumbling partners, dashed expectations, and smeared mascara. We didn't mean to mess up the dance. We didn't intend to leave the dance floor early. We didn't plan on spinning into the arms of a different partner. We didn't mean to screw it up so badly.

When we were children, our families were our first dance partners, and our home was the dance floor. They showed us a certain way to dance, and that way became familiar to us. It may not have been loving, enjoyable, skilled, or functional, but it was what we knew. Because we have imperfect families with imperfect parents, the dance got messy. Some of us even swore as youths, "I'll never be like them when I grow up!"

As adults, however, we unwittingly attract the same kind of dance partners to our adult dance floor. They may not look the same or act the same, but they *dance* the same. They *feel* the same. We put ourselves in the same position we were always in, and we repeat the same messy dance that our parents taught us. Sometimes we turn into the very person we swore we never would. Sometimes we *marry* the type of person who most hurt us as children. Sometimes we attract relationships that will only cause us more of the same kind of pain. It's almost as if we are addicted to the abuse and we don't see a different way.

Without God's intervention, the dance is just rhythm-less noise and chaotic movement. But God wants something better for you.

God wants your relationship to be the fluid, intimate, beautiful dance it was intended to be. He wants people to watch you dance and be filled with warmth and life and inspiration. But how? How do you stop attracting the wrong type of dance partner? How do you become the type of dance partner who makes a dance beautiful? How do you stop stepping on your partner and stop getting stepped on?

If you have been deeply wounded by the dance, I get it. Maybe your childhood family system set you up for what looked like a mosh pit instead of a dance floor. Maybe your childhood family system looked like a middle school dance in the gym. The boys lined up on one side and the girls lined up on the other, no one dared get close, and the "bad kids" made out behind the bleachers. Your family may have perceived it to be wrong and weak to want closeness, so you had to get it in ways that seemed taboo. Or maybe your childhood family system was touch and go, hot and cold, unpredictable and chaotic. Families with addictions and mental illness can feel intensely bipolar when love and war exist in the same breath. No matter what type of dance floor you used to learn your first steps, you can relearn what you need to know for healthy, loving relationships today.

· ·

Families with addictions and mental illness can feel intensely bipolar when love and war exist in the same breath.

· ·

The next section will take a closer look at the Facts. The Facts will show you what you need, what happens when you don't get what you need, and how to learn new dance steps to make your relationship beautiful.

Fact #1: It's not Love without the Vital Three: To be Seen, Known and Accepted Unconditionally

The deep desire of every human being is to be seen, known, and accepted. Like a dry sponge, the soul needs saturation, which it receives from authentic love. Only then can it become what it was meant to be. Below you will find the 411 on the Vital Three. You'll see how the Vital Three can be met in healthy ways. First, I'll give you a working definition of each vital concept. Then, I'll give one example of what each concept looks like between a parent and a child. Finally, I'll give one example of what each concept looks like between couples.

Vital Three #1: To Be Seen

To be **seen** is to be valued, recognized as a worthwhile individual, to be identified as uniquely separate with personal rights, needs, and interests equal to others; to be noticed, counted, and taken interest in. Significance has less to do with performance and behavior, and more to do with inherent human value. It is being seen as human—not more than human like an idol or a god, and not less than human, like a servant or a slave.

When a mother sees her child as a valuable person, separate from herself, she is able to see and meet her child's specific needs. For instance, if the child is struggling with her parents' divorce, and acting out at school, the mother sees her child's pain as separate from her own, and can address it by asking for help from the school counselor, meeting with the teacher, or talking it through with the child. The mother communicates to her child, "I see you. You are important to me, I care that you are hurting. I'm here for you." Instead of drowning in her own pain, the mother sees her child as important enough to temporarily set her own needs aside and meet the needs of her child. How many times have divorced mothers dried their own eyes before the afternoon school bus arrives so they can give their happiest and healthiest selves to their children? This happens all the time, and it's an example of a mother **seeing** her child has important value and needs separate from her own.

Here's another example. A young woman and young man marry. The husband's job takes them across the country to start their life together. The wife is unable to find work in her field and becomes depressed. The husband sees the professional sacrifice she made to be with him, and offers to quit his job and move to another area where she can find acceptable work. She, in turn, feels that her needs are **seen** as important. She appreciates his gesture so much that she determines to stick it out where she is, so that he can continue his career path. Because she feels **seen**, valued, and cared for, she has the strength to continue her sacrifice with contentment. His love spurs some out-of-the-box creativity in her. She reinvents herself professionally, and they decide together to heavily invest in her new business start-up. Her unique needs are seen, prioritized, and resourced. She feels **seen as a valuable person**.

Vital Three #2: To Be Known

To be **known** is to be understood. Knowing means perceiving, seeking, finding, and joining. Knowing involves being exposed, unguarded, and vulnerable, leading to intimate knowledge. *Knowing* is so deep and intimate, the ancient biblical scribes used the words, "to know" as a Hebrew idiom for sexual intercourse between a man and a woman. Knowing is not just understanding; it is also joining. Knowing is seeing another person completely exposed, with no secret feeling, flaw, or fear hidden.

For example, a father of two boys has an easier time bonding with his oldest son because they have so much in common. They enjoy watching football, playing catch, and all things traditionally "male." However, the father and his younger son are very different. The youngest son enjoys art, drama, and reading. He's smaller, less physically coordinated, and less athletic than his brother, and seems to get hurt easily. The youngest son feels inferior. The father sees the differences between the two boys, and although he has little natural interest in art, drama, and reading, he realizes that he must work harder to connect with his younger son. The father could routinely ask questions to engage his younger son, but won't find meaningful connection until he *joins with* the son in his interests. The father decides to register the two of them for an eight-week art class. The father begins to understand the boy's unique talent for art, and even discovers his own genuine interest in the subject. The father enjoys their new connection and looks for other ways the two of them can connect. The father sought greater understanding of his younger son, joined him in his interests and experiences, and communicated the message, "I love you and want to know you better." The son felt affirmed for his unique interests, became more self-confident, and had a deeper bond with his father. This is *knowing*.

Here is an example of what **knowing** looks like in marriage. Brian and Becky have been married for twelve years. They are compatible, committed, and caring toward one another but struggle to resolve conflict in a healthy way. She says she doesn't like the way he drives. He says he drives fine, and she shouldn't be so reactive. She says that he drives erratically and too fast. She says that driving with him makes her feel anxious and panicky. He says he can't stand it when she criticizes his driving.

After a short stalemate, Becky decides to take a different approach. She says, "OK, you are not a bad driver. You're actually a really good driver. We just have different driving styles. I get anxious when I'm in the passenger's seat because I feel out of control. When you speed up or stop short, I feel unsafe. My heart races, my adrenaline fires, and I start to have a panic attack. These attacks are terrible. My anxiety may not seem reasonable to you, but it is really painful to me."

Brian countered, "Yeah, but I'm not doing anything to threaten you. I'm just driving the way I normally do. Your freaking out in the front seat doesn't make anything better."

Silence.

"Brian, I'm telling you that I can't help it. I can't control my reaction to your driving. When it scares me, it scares me. I want you to consider my feelings on this. I don't know why I freak out like I do. Maybe it was the way my dad drove all the time. He'd yell and swerve and drive like a crazy man. I always felt scared riding with him when I was growing up."

More silence.

"Yeah, your dad *is* a crazy driver," Brian said with a knowing smile. "OK, I understand. When I see you're having a hard time, I'll try to slow down. Or better yet, why don't you just drive? Then you can give *me* panic attacks." They both smiled.

Brian put his hand on Becky's knee and said, "I'm sorry my driving scares you. I'll try to be more considerate."

Becky said, "I'm sorry I criticize your driving. I'll try to tell you what I need. Or I'll just drive."

Becky took a risk that paid off. She made herself vulnerable by admitting her own weakness and pain. Instead of attacking Brian's ability to drive, she humbly owned her anxious feelings. She talked about where they come from and how they feel, without blaming Brian for them. Brian joined with her pain with the simple statement, "Yeah, your dad *is* a crazy driver." That communicated validation for her feelings. He offered support and even a solution. He didn't shame her for her feelings; instead, he listened with care and concern. Both left the conversation with a deeper sense of knowing one another's vulnerabilities, fears, and weaknesses.

Vital Three #3: To Accepted Unconditionally

To be **accepted unconditionally** is to be loved; to be received willingly, given favor, and have the best believed of you. Even when you mess up, make mistakes, and hurt the people around you, you are given the opportunity to be accepted back into relationship. To be accepted is to feel genuinely liked, with a sense of belonging. Being accepted means you are free to be you, with no threat of purposeful abandonment or smothering control.[5]

For example, imagine a child who is struggling to read and write, who takes several hours every night to complete her homework. Her parents are frustrated with her lack of progress and tell their daughter to pay better attention in class. Neither of them remember struggling in school, so they assume their daughter must not be trying hard enough. They soon discover that cajoling, lecturing, and more discipline are ineffective, so they do the humble thing: change tactics and seek outside help. (Yay for humble parents!) The child is diagnosed with an attention disorder and severe learning challenges. Once the parents accept the diagnosis and try various ADHD treatments, they

---

5   Men may choose to replace the word acceptance with respect. In this case, both acceptance and respect are demonstrations of love; however, respect is typically more important to men. Respect is just another form of acceptance.

start to see major improvements in their daughter's reading and writing ability, not to mention a big spike in her self-esteem.

The parents could have let pride blind them into thinking, "No child of mine has issues!" But instead of forcing their child to conform to unrealistic expectations, the parents adjusted their expectations to meet reality, and accepted their child as is. In effect, the parents' message became, "You are not bad for having challenges; you are human. We love you no matter what and we'll work as a team to overcome our challenges."

This experience is a learning curve for the parents as well as the child. The child learns that personal quirks, challenges, and special needs are not reasons to be rejected or embarrassed; they are just part of being human. The parents learn that admitting failure and accepting help is the best and often the *only* way to improve! The parents have the power to show unconditional acceptance to their child, no matter the challenge. This gives the child safety to be unique, creative, and confident.

Gerri and Rob have been married for two years. Since that time, Gerri has struggled with her mood and her weight. Gerri's mother died unexpectedly during the first year of their marriage, and Gerri hasn't fully recovered. Gerri feels lonely and hopeless much of the time. She thinks she should feel happy with her marriage but doesn't know how to change the way she feels. She binges on chips and ice cream when Rob is at work and then hides the evidence because of the guilt she feels. When Rob finally brings up the moodiness and weight gain, she is overwhelmed with shame. He wisely says, "I love you, and I'm worried that you are getting worse instead of better. You're not the same person I married. You used to be fun and talkative. I want you to be happy again. I miss you." Gerri sighs with relief over Rob's tenderness. She expected him to be angry about her failures, but his loving kindness helps her to relax.

Because she feels cared for instead of judged, she makes a brave choice to trust Rob's intentions and open up to him. She shares her fears, her grief, and the intense shame she feels about her emotional eating. Rob comforts her by saying, "I love you just the way you are. I understand how this can be overwhelming. I'm not mad at you, and I'm not judging you. But, I do think it's okay to get some help to work through it. Would you be willing to get some help? We can do what it takes to afford it." Gerri accepts some grief counseling and slowly notices improvements in her mood and eating behaviors. Gerri experiences unconditional acceptance, even in the face of weakness and shame. This unconditional acceptance helps her to take the necessary steps toward happiness and wholeness.

To Recap:

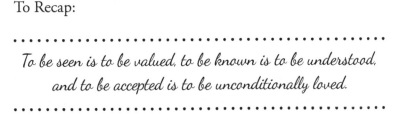

To be seen is to be valued, to be known is to be understood, and to be accepted is to be unconditionally loved.

Now that you have a solid understanding of the Vital Three and their importance in relationship health, let's see how Soul Holes form.

Fact #2: If the Vital Three are not met, Soul Holes Grow

Soul Holes are emotional wounds inflicted by imperfect people with imperfect love. *Soul Holes are caused by anything less than nurturing when nurturing was called for.*

Soul Holes can be "little-t" traumas that happened throughout the growing up years, "big-T" traumas that happen on occasion, or a combination of both. Think of this for a moment: every time you were called a name at school, or you sat frightened and alone in your room, or you witnessed adult rage or inappropriate sexual content, or you were shoved by older kids on the bus, all of those things had traumatizing effects on your developing self. Anything less than the Vital Three will cause Soul Holes.

Even the best of parents can't meet all their children's needs all the time, or avoid failing or hurting them. Unfortunately, you may not say that you had the best of parents. Maybe you feel the nicest thing you can say about your parents is that they showed you how *not* to be. If you were not **seen, known,** and **unconditionally accepted** growing up, then you are familiar with feeling invisible, alone, and unacceptable. Maybe instead of being seen, you are more familiar with feeling marginalized, de-valued, and discounted. Maybe instead of being known and understood, you felt misunderstood, thought the worst of, and ashamed. Maybe instead of being accepted, you felt judged, rejected, or abandoned.

The needs to be **seen, known,** and **accepted** don't just go away when we become adults. They go underground, just under our aware-ness, until something like a significant love relationship opens them up again. Love relationships have a way of exposing our Soul Holes just enough to make life painful. In fact, research shows that women who were sexually abused as children are more likely to be sexually or physically abused in their marriages.[6] Because trauma lodges itself so powerfully in the brain and psyche, the victim unconsciously rehearses the traumatization later in life with new partners, like an unconscious script directing her toward new traumatizing relation-ships. A number of researchers have observed that re-traumatization

---

6   Russell DEH: *The Secret Trauma: Incest in the Lives of Girls and Women.* New York, Basic Books, 1986

and re-victimization of people who have experienced trauma, especially trauma in childhood, are an all too common phenomena.[7] That's how we know we have some Soul Holes to heal.

To explain Soul Holes in another way, they are like wounds and are similar to physical wounds, except you can't see them. A person injured in a car accident may take weeks or months to heal from the various injuries caused by the force and impact. They may need casts, stitches, crutches, and surgeries to recover. Even though medical attention helps a lot, spines and necks and bones don't always return to pain-free, normal functioning. Soul Holes, like physical wounds, take time and attention to heal properly, too.

Soul holes are a result of unmet needs. Even if the wounding was not intentional, malicious, or abusive, the unmet need remains just that—unmet. If your core needs are not met early in life, a vacuum is created with a bottomless pit. This vacuum sucks, attracts, and draws in anything that promises to fill it up.

Some of the deepest holes in life come from experiences like:

- opening yourself to love, and then being rejected, used, or betrayed
- trusting someone and being used, abused, or taken advantage of
- loving someone and then losing him/her to death, divorce, or estrangement
- trusting someone, and then being slandered, exposed, blamed, or attacked
- depending on a parent who lets you down, shames you, or uses you for their own purposes

7   Browne A, Finkelhor D: Impact of child sexual abuse: a review of the literature. *Psychol Bull* 1986;99:66–77 [PubMed]

This list evokes the kind of deeply felt pain that words can't accurately describe. Without proper attention to these Soul Holes, the empty and injured are set in a pattern of attracting more pain and more injury to themselves.

Fact #3: Soul Holes attract Losers, Users, and Abusers

The remainder of this book will help you identify what kind of people you attract and how to attract authentic love instead. Depending on your core unmet needs of being **seen**, **known**, and **accepted**, you will attract certain types of people in hopes of filling those needs. You will attract the same type of person who originally injured you, unconsciously hoping against all hope that this time you'll be able to get the love you need. The problem is the type of person you keep attracting is completely unable to give you what you need. You unwittingly re-enact the trauma of the past in the present, causing more pain and trauma to yourself. If you have Soul Holes, you will attract Losers, Users, and Abusers.

Hannah's Story

For example, Hannah was the oldest of four children and raised by an alcoholic mother. When her mother was in a long stretch of sobriety, she was attentive, hard-working, and available. But when she began drinking again, she was irresponsible, depressed, and checked out. Hannah became the responsible mother figure to her siblings, showed up to work for her mom, and cleaned up the messes. In adulthood, Hannah felt drawn to men who were emotionally unavailable. They were either obsessed with their work, or their friends, or themselves. She repeatedly became involved with men who took her generosity, care, and devotion for granted. She was so used to being the "the responsible one in the relationship" as a child, she naturally took the responsible role with the men she dated. Emotionally irresponsible men loved dating Hannah, because they didn't have to do any of the relationship work. Hannah did all the caring, calling, helping, listening, understanding, and nurturing. She even paid off the car note for one of her boyfriends, because his "upset over the debt kept him from getting a job." She was trying to make emotionally unavailable men emotionally connect with her. She was trying to get love from the same ole' empty well and found it was still empty. Her unmet need to be *seen* as valuable drove her toward men who *used* her.

In this book, I'll be giving many examples that explain the relationship between your signature Soul Holes and the type of people you attract. Identifying your signature Soul Holes and learning to meet your Vital Three needs in healthy ways will set you up for real love.

No human is whole unless the Vital Three are fully met. When they are met, you will notice that things will change for you. You will naturally give yourself love and respect. Your pesky insecurities will lose their grip. You will know what you need and how to meet your needs. You will be content with who you are as a person and be able to accept others. You won't look to people to do for you what only God can do. You'll have an abiding sense that you are not alone and that God is with you and for you. You'll be able to set boundaries with those who use or abuse you. You'll notice that you attract Lovers instead of Losers. Since you will have received God's love in tangible ways, you'll begin to attract authentic love to yourself. You will affect change in your relationships for the better. You'll be able to forgive Losers, set healthy boundaries with Users, avoid Abusers, and attract Authentic Lovers. You will attract Real Love to yourself.

Fact #4: Soul Holes fill by being Seen, Known, and Accepted Unconditionally

I know a thing or two about filling holes. Ever since our dog dug out of the backyard and discovered the unleashed joys of cavorting through the neighborhood, I've had my fill of shoveling dirt. Affectionately referred to as "The Beast," our black lab is 105 pounds of unstoppable, indomitable, digging power. Chicken wire, shock collar, cement posts—they mean nothing to him. Dirt, stumps, and stones fly with ferocious abandon as he makes his way toward freedom.

The Beast is a friendly escapee, however. He runs full speed toward walkers unaware, all tongue and teeth, and dripping drool, just to make a new friend. He runs up on small carefree children walking home from school, and makes them cry. The children leave terrifying encounters with bruises from The Beast's incessant heavy tail whapping.

Nearly every neighbor in a mile radius has rescued The Beast off the street, called the number on his tags, and asked the question, "Are you missing your dog?"

Missing? Is that a trick question? How would you define *missing* exactly? We're tempted to reply, "Not really, why? Do you want him?"

The holes that my dog digs take sweat, effort, and a good deal of cursing to fill properly. Figuring out how to fill them cleverly, so as to outwit The Beast, takes thoughtful planning, patience, and tenacity.

The same fortitude is needed to fill Soul Holes with authentic love. There will be times that your efforts at healing seem useless and you feel powerless over your past. You will feel frustrated with your progress. You'll feel like the pain and betrayal are too raw, too overwhelming, and too pervasive to overcome. The bible warns, "In this world you will have trouble," so it is reasonable to expect the journey toward wholeness and happiness to be challenging. But Jesus says, "Take heart! I have overcome the world." [8] With God's help, Soul Holes can be filled, authentic love can be experienced, and your relationships can be happy. The result, a whole life, is worth the effort you put into it!

You must meet your Vital Three to Fill your Soul Holes.

Each time you recognize and verbalize one of your Vital Three needs, you throw a little dirt in the hole. Each time you say "no" to something or someone who is sucking you dry, you throw a little dirt in the hole. Each time you refuse to be hard on yourself, and instead offer yourself some grace, you throw a little dirt in the hole. When you trust God for your self-worth, you're shoveling dirt. With all that practice, you will become a proficient dirt shoveler, and you'll have the guns (and the aching back) to prove it. One day, you'll look up from shoveling, and you'll be astonished at all the flowers God has planted in the holes around you. Your hard work is just beautiful!

Fact #5: The Vital Three Start with You

Speaking of guns, let's give those soul muscles a little ammunition. Muscles need exercise to do what we want them to do. My leg muscles are good for walking, standing, and occasionally a little running. But if I wanted to compete in a 10k race, I would need to give my legs some extra exercise to get them ready. Maintaining the status quo for your relationship won't take much effort—your relationship muscles can already do that. But, if you want to fill your Soul Holes

---

8   Jn 16:33 (New International Version).

and *strengthen* your relationships, you will need to exercise your relationship muscles.

Relationship Exercises—it's all in the REPS

Relationship REPS are an acronym for:

R **R**estore order through boundaries (taking care of yourself while respecting others.)

E **E**xperience God (reconnecting spiritually for help, guidance and self-worth.)

P **P**rovide yourself with people (connecting with supportive people with love and belonging.)

S **S**eek intimacy (authentically responding to others with vulnerability and goodwill.)

Relationship REPS will be included at the end of the chapter so you have sustainable action steps that you can start doing right away to change your relationships for the better.

Are you eager to get started and find out where your relationships are at on the LULA (Lovers, Losers, Users, and Abusers) Quadrant? Are you wondering what kind of relationship you attract most often and why? Are you eager to find out how to attract Authentic Love and avoid Losers, Users, and Abusers? Let's get started!

Chapter 3

Let the LULA be the Rula'!

*"The curious paradox is that when I accept myself just as I am,
then I can change."*

—*Carl R. Rogers*

"I thought I was doing so well. But this last month, I've had a lot more anxiety than usual. It's like a monster who keeps following me, and I can't get away from it." Rebecca was a recent college grad in between jobs, still deciding on a career path, and living with her parents. She had been in counseling for a few months about a year before, working on anxious feelings and catastrophic thinking. Now she was back, and, apparently, so was her anxiety.

I asked her, "What changed? What has happened over the last few weeks that caused your anxiety to spike?"

Rebecca twisted in her seat and listed some recent events like job interviews, a minor falling out with her sister, and paying back her student loans. But then her expression changed, her eyes lowered, and her brow furrowed just a bit. If I had blinked, I would have missed the shadow that crossed her face. She said, "I'm seeing this guy, Andrew. He's my older sister's friend from college. He has a lot going for him, like his own place, a great job, a nice car, and I think he really likes me. But I'm not sure how I feel about him. I met him for the first time a couple years back, and I thought he was an arrogant jerk, totally full of himself. But now I see the nicer side of him. He takes me nice places, helps me plan my finances better. He's super smart. He seems really great now."

I gingerly asked, "So, what's the problem?" Already, I was interested in the complicated and mysterious Andrew—the Arrogant Jerk with the Nicer Side. I wondered quietly which one was the real one? I was even more interested by the inner conflict Rebecca was having. The two sides of Andrew were giving Rebecca some misgivings. Rightfully so.

"Well," Rebecca pondered aloud. "I'm not sure, except that I feel confused."

"Confusion can cause anxiety. Starting a new romantic relationship should be fun, and even a little exciting. So, let's figure out why you feel confused instead."

Once we met a few more times, Rebecca discovered a few things about herself, and a few things about Andrew that helped her see her relationship more clearly. She identified her needs, and recognized the importance of verbalizing them. Even though it was uncomfortable to do so, verbalizing her needs and wants to Andrew gave her a great sense of self-empowerment and relief from the anxiety she was feeling. Whether she stays with Andrew remains to be seen, but Rebecca can now recognize and legitimize her needs as important. If Andrew does not see them this way, then Rebecca knows there is a mismatch.

The next section will help you do the same. Even if you've been married for years, accepting where your relationship is will help you determine your next steps.

THE LULA QUADRANT

The LULA Quadrant is an acronym for Lovers, Losers, Users, and Abusers, and it is designed to help you recognize and legitimize your needs, and identify your healthy and unhealthy relationships. The LULA Quadrant will help you with all your relationships, not just your romantic one. You can use it to help you with your aging parents, your children, your boss, and your friends.

No relationship fits perfectly in a tight square box because relationships are fluid. They grow and morph. They change with seasons, pressures, demands, and time. However, the LULA Quadrant will help you think about your core needs to be seen, known, and accepted; how those needs are being met or not met; and the type of relationships in which you participate currently.

So go on, take a look. Let the LULA be the Rula' by which you measure your relationship needs and standards.

LOVER RELATIONSHIPS	LOSER RELATIONSHIPS
Lovers *see* you as a valuable and separate individual. Lovers *know*, understand you, and *accept* you just as you are. Lovers make you feel genuinely valued as a unique human being with a voice and your own point of view. Lovers give privilege, exclusive access to intimate knowledge of him/herself. Lovers make you comfortable to share weaknesses and failures without fear of shame. Lovers see all of you with affection and extend freedom to be yourself. They love you unconditionally. *You are Seen, Known, and Accepted Unconditionally*	Losers *see* you as valuable and separate with unique and valid needs, but they don't *know* you because they fear the vulnerability of intimacy. Instead of connecting, they hide their fears, weaknesses, and true feelings, sometimes denying they have any. Because they don't know themselves, they cannot know or love you fully either. They are emotionally distant or absent. This is the most common quadrant in relationships because people naturally resist emotional intimacy. Facing the fear of intimacy can help turn your Loser into a Lover. *You are Seen, Unknown, and Accepted with Condition*
USER RELATIONSHIPS	ABUSER RELATIONSHIPS
Users do not *see* you because they are too fixated on their own needs. You are not a valuable and separate individual, but a tool. They will make you feel *known* and understood, but that is because they study you like a salesman studies a prospect. Instead of being fully accepted and loved, you are controlled for their interest. Users do not bond or share for any reason other than to use you. Users won't mean harm, but they are careless because they are selfish. Users seek people who keep them on a pedestal. This is an unhealthy relationship that needs serious boundaries and support. *You are Unseen, Known, and Selfishly Used*	Abusers are tricky little devils. No pun intended. They *see* you and *know* you but their affection is *false*. The difference between Users and Abusers is Malice. You are seen and valued in order to be controlled. They value keeping you because they need you to prop them up. You are known to gain your allegiance. They deal in confusion, making you to feel wanted and hated all at the same time. Abusers are malicious and often will stop at nothing to stay in control of you. Abuser Relationships are toxic and dangerous. Expert support is needed to become safe and ultimately free of their abuse. *You are Seen, Known, and Maliciously Controlled*

Different Relationships, Different Quadrants

You weave an elegant, yet complicated web of connections throughout your life. The strong ties of love bond you with people, family, and friends. Some are more distant than others, but the heart bonds are still strong. The LULA Quadrant is a means of seeing and categorizing those connections, so you can strengthen yourself and your relationships.

Relationship Fluidity

Relationships are fluid, not fixed, so you may find your marriage seemed more in the LOVER Quadrant in the beginning, but ten years later, it feels like it's in the LOSER Quadrant. That's okay. Relationships change with environmental pressures (jobs, moves, family deaths) and stage of life pressures (raising children and caring for elderly parents). The relationships in your life will mature, grow closer, and grow apart. With some self-awareness, time, and focused effort, the goal is to move all your relationships closer to the LOVER Quadrant. You can do it!

· ·

There is one caveat with the Abuser Quadrant: abuser relationships are not for FIXING; they are for ESCAPING.

· ·

We'll talk more about this later in the book.

Labels

Your relationships are complex and multifaceted and much more that can fit in a square box. But the LULA Quadrant is useful as a simple way to see and understand relationships. The LULA Quadrant is a way to *see* and *change* your relationships, so long as you don't *reduce* your relationships to labels only. Your relationships may have overlap and similarities with other quadrants, but you will find each relationship falls predominantly in one. So, let the LULA be the Rula! Let it be the ruler by which you measure your relationship standards, and a guide to help you create the strong and happy relationships you want.

SELF-ASSESSMENT

It is essential to be as self-aware as possible when reading through this chapter. Your self-awareness is the most important asset you have in assessing the health of your relationships. Don't be afraid of what you might find. The truth is your friend, so be honest when you're answering these questions. You know the kind of friend that you feel comfortable with even without make-up, before coffee, and while you're still in your bathrobe? Let TRUTH be that kind of friend. It may be tempting to fudge the answers and make reality prettier than it actually is, but it won't help you in the long run.

These questions are to help you assess where in the LULA Quadrant your relationships currently reside. These are simple yes-or-no questions designed to give you specific examples of healthy vs. unhealthy relationship characteristics. It will be difficult to answer some questions either "yes" or "no" because you'll want to answer "sometimes." Relationships are not ALL one way or ALL the other way. They are not black and white; they are different shades of gray. But, to simplify the scoring process, please answer the questions either "yes, often" or "no, not really" without use of qualifiers. At the end of the assessment, you'll have a general overview of your relationship health. Answer the first way that comes to mind and try not to overthink the question. Move through the assessment quickly. The number of affirmative answers will give you an idea of where your significant relationships dwell.

LOVERS QUADRANT:

		Yes, often	No, not really
1.	Do you and your partner fight fair? (listening without interruption, using "I feel" language while avoiding generalizations, yelling, cussing, name-calling.)	☐	☐
2.	Do you and your partner share equal (though not necessarily the same) relationship responsibilities and privileges (household chores, earning income, initiating alone time, lovemaking, child rearing, bookkeeping, cooking)?	☐	☐
3.	Does your significant other support you verbally and/or participate when training your children?	☐	☐
4.	Do you share similar values on spending/saving money?	☐	☐
5.	Do you share similar values on work ethic, motivation, and ambition?	☐	☐
6.	Do you share similar values on child rearing and elder care, if applicable?	☐	☐
7.	Do you share similar values on religious faith and practice?	☐	☐
8.	Do you prioritize and schedule routine time together doing activities you and your partner mutually enjoy?	☐	☐
9.	Are you free to be yourself without fear of judgment or excessive criticism?	☐	☐
10.	Do you and your significant other attempt conflict resolution with positive results more times than not?	☐	☐

11. Do you feel appreciated?

Yes, often ☐   No, not really ☐

12. Do you feel safe expressing intimate feelings, hopes, and fears with your significant other, knowing he will keep that information private?

Yes, often ☐   No, not really ☐

13. Can your significant other be vulnerable with you, exposing things that have been a source of embarrassment or shame?

Yes, often ☐   No, not really ☐

14. Do you know how to listen reflectively to your partner without jumping in to fix, defend, or criticize?

Yes, often ☐   No, not really ☐

15. Do you and your significant other re-establish connection after a fight with positive regard, a humble apology, overt forgiveness, and heartfelt affection?

Yes, often ☐   No, not really ☐

16. Do you like each other?

Yes, often ☐   No, not really ☐

17. Do you and your significant other work together to achieve common goals?

Yes, often ☐   No, not really ☐

18. Do you and your partner laugh easily and often?

Yes, often ☐   No, not really ☐

19. Is your significant other unembarrassed and unencumbered to show affection to you in public (hand holding, light kiss, dancing together)?

Yes, often ☐   No, not really ☐

20. Are you free to say "no" in your relationship without fear of being guilted, shamed, or blamed? In other words, are your boundaries respected?

Yes, often ☐   No, not really ☐

LOSERS QUADRANT:

1. Do you feel more like a roommate with your partner than a spouse or lover?

   Yes, often ☐   *No, not really* ☐

2. Does your sex life feel stale, more like a duty or obligation than an act of love and passion?

   Yes, often ☐   *No, not really* ☐

3. Is your partner more passive and/or explosive when it comes to training your children?

   Yes, often ☐   *No, not really* ☐

4. Do you and your partner routinely have unresolved conflict?

   Yes, often ☐   *No, not really* ☐

5. Do you have dissimilar values on spending/saving money?

   Yes, often ☐   *No, not really* ☐

6. Do you have dissimilar values on work ethic, motivation, and ambition?

   Yes, often ☐   *No, not really* ☐

7. Do you have dissimilar values on child rearing and elder care, if applicable?

   Yes, often ☐   *No, not really* ☐

8. Do you have dissimilar values on religious faith and practice?

   Yes, often ☐   *No, not really* ☐

9. Does your significant other roll his eyes, say, "not again," or shut down when you say, "Can we talk?"

   Yes, often ☐   *No, not really* ☐

10. Does your significant other refuse to show intense emotion like crying or laughing? Is the only acceptable intense emotion anger?

    Yes, often ☐   *No, not really* ☐

11. Do you or your partner pretend that everything is okay when around other people, but feel like strangers when you're together?

Yes, often ☐   *No, not really* ☐

12. When your significant other shares or experiences something that makes him feel vulnerable, do you feel uncomfortable, make a joke to ease the tension, or pick a fight to evade intimacy?

Yes, often ☐   *No, not really* ☐

13. Do you long for emotional intimacy with your significant other, but don't know what it looks like, feels like, or how to get it?

Yes, often ☐   *No, not really* ☐

14. When you share a problem with your significant other, does he say, "You shouldn't feel that way," or tell you how to solve your problem?

Yes, often ☐   *No, not really* ☐

15. Do either you or your partner create an argument or crisis just to feel some emotional intensity in the place of the relational dullness or distance?

Yes, often ☐   *No, not really* ☐

16. Do you avoid difficult conversations because of fear of conflict, fear of feeling rejected, ignored, or stalemated?

Yes, often ☐   *No, not really* ☐

17. Are you or your significant other guilty of being overly judgmental or critical, making it unsafe to be emotionally vulnerable?

Yes, often ☐   *No, not really* ☐

18. Do you or your significant other become defensive or shutdown when a sensitive topic comes up?

Yes, often ☐   *No, not really* ☐

19. Do you or your partner prioritize work, kids, other activities over your relationship?

Yes, often ☐   *No, not really* ☐

20. Does your busy schedule or lack of desire inhibit planning mutually enjoyable activities like date night?

Yes, often ☐   *No, not really* ☐

USERS

		Yes, often	No, not really
1.	Do your needs for sexual intimacy, safety, or comfort come second to his sexual needs or demands?	☐	☐
2.	Does your significant other make sure he is seen in a positive light with your children, even if it means painting you in a negative light?	☐	☐
3.	Does your partner flirt with attractive women, even when you're with him, and then deny it meant anything, and that it shouldn't bother you?	☐	☐
4.	Do you feel like your significant other is the biggest person in the relationship? That his needs are the biggest and most important, and that yours should take second place?	☐	☐
5.	Have you told your significant other private things in moments of emotional intimacy, thinking he was being understanding and sensitive, only to realize later that he used that private information for his own benefit?	☐	☐
6.	Do you feel like your partner cannot handle being wrong or admit to wrongdoing?	☐	☐
7.	Do you wonder if you mean as much to him as he means to you?	☐	☐
8.	Does your partner think he is better or smarter than you?	☐	☐
9.	Does your significant other act entitled to things like sex, obedience, or service that is inconvenient for you?	☐	☐

10. Do you feel coerced into doing or saying things you're uncomfortable with in order to make him happy?

Yes, often ☐   *No, not really* ☐

11. Does your partner's mood change unpredictably and abruptly, making you wonder what you did to cause it?

Yes, often ☐   *No, not really* ☐

12. Do you think other women have more confidence, are prettier, are smarter or more talented than you?

Yes, often ☐   *No, not really* ☐

13. Do you wonder if your significant other is telling you the truth, or the whole truth? Do you get a sense that he is hiding something?

Yes, often ☐   *No, not really* ☐

14. Does your significant other care incessantly about his public image and become pouty or angry when you say or do something that challenges that image?

Yes, often ☐   *No, not really* ☐

15. Do you feel like he is only there for you when it's convenient?

Yes, often ☐   *No, not really* ☐

16. Does he make promises he doesn't keep? Keeping you hooked with new promises?

Yes, often ☐   *No, not really* ☐

17. Does your significant other make excuses or blame other people for his bad behavior?

Yes, often ☐   *No, not really* ☐

18. Does your significant other speak with such authority that you find yourself questioning your own motives, abilities, or intelligence?

Yes, often ☐   *No, not really* ☐

19. Does your significant other use or abuse alcohol, drugs, or pornography regularly to alter his mood?

Yes, often ☐   *No, not really* ☐

ABUSERS QUADRANT:

		Yes, often	*No, not really*
1.	Has your partner physically forced or psychologically manipulated you to have sex with him?	☐	☐
2.	Is child rearing left up to you, unless the responsibility somehow strokes his ego, puts him in a positive light with others, or is abusive in nature? Are child rearing duties defined, authorized and carried out according to his requirements?	☐	☐
3.	Does your partner flirt with other women, or even cheat on you, but insist that it isn't a big deal, that men have certain natural needs, and that you're the one with the problem, not him?	☐	☐
4.	Has your partner used money against you, lied about financial failures, or put your financial security at risk?	☐	☐
5.	Does your significant other criticize or belittle you about your religious faith and practices, or lack thereof?	☐	☐
6.	Have you told your significant other private things in moments of emotional intimacy, thinking he was understanding and sensitive, only to realize later that he used that private information against you?	☐	☐
7.	Do you feel like your significant other is two different people? Mr. Nice guy in public, but downright mean to you in private?	☐	☐
8.	Do you ever fear that someday he might really hurt you or the kids?	☐	☐
9.	Has your partner struggled with addictions, habitual lying, or criminal activity?	☐	☐

10. Do you find yourself making excuses for his bad behavior, like, "He's been working so hard lately," or "He had a really bad childhood," or "If I wouldn't have set him off, he wouldn't have exploded?"

Yes, often ☐   *No, not really* ☐

11. Do you feel like all your fights are somehow your fault?

Yes, often ☐   *No, not really* ☐

12. Do you feel compelled to stay with him because he is insecure, because he needs you, or because you're the only one who truly understands him?

Yes, often ☐   *No, not really* ☐

13. Do you feel compelled to stay with him because you are afraid he would hurt you, hurt someone you love, or threaten suicide if you left him?

Yes, often ☐   *No, not really* ☐

14. Do you ever find yourself thinking, "If I just do what he is asking me to do, everything will be all right, and he won't get so angry?"

Yes, often ☐   *No, not really* ☐

15. Does your partner control the money, giving you instruction on what you can or cannot buy?

Yes, often ☐   *No, not really* ☐

16. Have you experienced him calling you horrible names, putting you down, and judging your motives or your IQ?

Yes, often ☐   *No, not really* ☐

17. Do you feel suffocated, smothered, controlled, or spied on?

Yes, often ☐   *No, not really* ☐

18. Do you wonder if your significant other is always telling you the truth, or the whole truth? Do you get a sense that he is hiding something?

Yes, often ☐   *No, not really* ☐

19. Does your significant other get your family and/or friends to turn against you, believing him instead of you?

Yes, often ☐   *No, not really* ☐

20. Do you continually second-guess yourself, question your memory, or feel like you're going crazy?

Yes, often ☐   *No, not really* ☐

Scoring Yourself

Now, add up the number of *yes* responses in each LULA section. You'll have a number for the Lovers Quadrant, the Losers Quadrant, the Users Quadrant, and the Abusers Quadrant. Whichever quadrant you scored the highest in is the quadrant your relationship is *currently* in.

LOVERS SCORE _____

LOSERS SCORE _____

USERS SCORE _____

ABUSERS SCORE _____

How are you doing? Did you experience some difficult feelings while you were answering the questions? You are not alone. This powerful tool is difficult for everyone to get through, because it illustrates your relationship reality. Facing reality can be a powerful awakening that sometimes causes doubts, fears, and disappointments. Perhaps you are wondering if you've made a mistake, or if it's too late to change things. Many women feel overwhelmed with the unknowns, the hard feelings, and the hard road ahead.

Feel those feelings all the way through, but don't let the dust settle on them. You don't have to solve all the problems or unknowns today. You must only take one small step at a time. You must make one small choice at a time, one moment, and one day at a time. You will know what you need to do, when you need to do it. And this book will help you.

I don't recommend you show your answers to your partner, as these answers are for you to process in your own timing. This book is not about changing your partner or getting a response from him, as much as it is about helping you to change from the inside out.

The feelings that you now experience after taking the assessment are normal and okay. You are okay, too. You will likely be thinking about your answers for a while. When you are ready, start reading the section that is most relevant to you, and then move to the other chapters. You will find a thorough investigation of each quadrant in the next four chapters, replete with stories, examples, and strategies to turn you and your relationships around. You will find *simple* tools that will make *extraordinary* differences in your relationships. You can start experiencing improvement *today*.

Chapter 4

Losers: You Can Look, But You Can't Touch

"Most people are slow to champion love because they fear the transformation it brings into their lives. And make no mistake about it: love does take over and transform the schemes and operations of our egos in a very mighty way."

—*Aberjhani*

Rebecca and Tim had been married for two years and lived in the suburbs close to Tim's job. Tim worked for a company that engineered airplanes, and Rebecca, who started low on the ladder at a marketing firm, had already been promoted. Tim saw Rebecca as a smart, pretty woman who was self-sufficient, and he loved her.

They shared household responsibilities like paying bills and cleaning house, and they liked similar hobbies. Tim commented that he was glad she wasn't like some of the girls he dated—girls that were too emotional and dramatic. He didn't like to have "deep conversations" and talk about feelings. He married Rebecca because she was different that way. Rebecca prided herself as being "just what Tim needed," and their arrangement worked. Sure, there wasn't a lot of emotional intimacy. No opening up about fears or hurts. No crying on each other's shoulders when something bad happened at work. But neither of them were really into that anyway. Or at least that's what Rebecca told herself.

One night, Rebecca caught Tim taking secretive phone calls in the garage. At first, Rebecca didn't press him because she didn't want to appear as though she didn't trust Tim. She thought, "I don't want to start a fight, so I will give him space." Rebecca continued to act as though nothing was wrong, making the bed in the morning, leaving for work with a hug and a kiss, and scheduling a tee time for them on Saturday.

A couple weeks went by, and, as the private phone calls continued, Rebecca's anxiety peaked. She felt ashamed of herself for being angry. "Really, I should trust him more," she'd say to calm herself. One Sunday afternoon, when she could not control her fears any longer, she burst into the garage and screamed, "Who is she? Let me have the phone!"

Tim, shocked and speechless, slowly handed the phone to Rebecca, where she heard the voice of Tim's mother shouting on the phone, "Tim, are you there? What happened?"

After some embarrassing apologies, Rebecca returned to the house, sullen and alone. She thought to herself that she actually wished it had been another woman—*anybody* but his mother. Always, his mother. Rebecca had shared her annoyance over Tim's mother before. The one time Rebecca complained to Tim about him spending too much time talking to his mother, he uncharacteristically lost his temper. The more Rebecca pressed, the angrier he got. With tears, she told him that she wished he would talk to her more, and open up more, be as close to her as he seemed with his mom.

Tim shouted, "Don't you start too! Everybody needs something from me! Why can't you just be happy! I give you everything I can, and it's never enough! My mother is fragile; how can you ask me to abandon her?"

That was the last time Rebecca shared her true feelings with Tim. She decided to just try to be the best wife she could be, without asking too much. She knew that Tim was a good man and that he loved her in his own way. He bought her gifts, complimented her, and came home every night for dinner. Maybe his mother really did need him more than she did. Maybe Rebecca was just being jealous and needed to get over it. But Rebecca couldn't shake the fear that Tim's mother was the third person in a marriage built only for two.

Tim's father was a long-haul truck driver and was rarely home while Tim grew up. When his dad was there, he didn't engage with the family much. Tim was the oldest of three kids and the only boy. In adolescence, Tim became a surrogate partner to his mother. She turned to him when she needed help parenting the other two children and when she needed a shoulder to cry on. She called him her "life support," and would say things like, "Tim's nothing like his father; he's always there for me."

When Rebecca and Tim got married, Tim had been glad that he found someone as "low maintenance" as Rebecca. She was so self-sufficient that she barely needed him at all.

Nearing the end of the third year of marriage, Rebecca resigned herself to be second. She knew that she had Tim's hand in marriage, his paycheck in the bank, and his body next to hers each night. But his heart belonged to one person, and that was his mother. Rebecca decided this was as good as it would get, and it would have to be good enough. She thought, *What I want doesn't really matter in this marriage.*

Rebecca was married to a Loser. Not a loser in the pop-cultural sense, the last kid picked for the team, or the couch potato in front of the television. Tim was a Loser because he lost out on truly knowing Rebecca.

He *saw* her, but didn't *know* her, and so could not truly *accept* her.

Tim saw her as a valuable person with unique gifts. He respected her and showed her commitment and responsibility. But he could not *know* her intimately because he was in love with someone else. Rebecca cut herself off from him after the first fight over his mother. She stopped believing that her need to be *known* was important, that emotional intimacy was even a possibility, and that her heart was as valuable as her head. She stopped trying to share her thoughts and feelings, and she stopped expecting that Tim should share his. Her thoughts and feelings went underground and stuck solidly, like an anchor in her stomach.

Ultimately, she felt unloved and desperately alone. They had friends over and got involved in social groups, but nobody knew how lonely she was. She put on the brave face of self-reliance and told herself she really shouldn't feel so alone. She had a good job with good people, she had a good husband, and she made a good living. She should be happy. This must be as good as it gets.

Seven years into the marriage, she met a man while traveling who seemed to make feelings she had long thought dead come back with force. She saw him every few months while away on quarterly business meetings, and, over time, they got to know each other. He listened to her, and he wanted to know more about her. She couldn't believe it, but she shared things with him that she had never told anyone. He opened up about his feelings too. She had desired to connect with someone for so long! She felt important, pursued, trusted, and, for the first time in a long time, she felt truly *known*. Like a ship setting sail, she was a woman set free and unfettered when she was with him. Even the guilt she had about the affair was not enough to keep her from seeing him. Her feelings, that had been locked up for so long, were like champagne uncorked.

She compartmentalized herself, split herself in two, and rationalized the affair as something she needed to keep her marriage together. She would lose everything in the end.

Her hidden romance carried on for a couple of years, but they saw each other less when he was promoted and changed regions. Rebecca knew he would never leave his wife, and they eventually grew distant. There was little keeping Tim and her together now. They seemed to live separate lives, and neither's heart was in the marriage. Eventually they divorced, amicably of course; there was never a cross word between them. There was nothing between them, in truth. Rebecca became the Loser too.

What happened? How did she get there? She wondered if she could ever be whole and happy again.

Most people *see* and respect their partners as valuable people, because that is the easy part. Showing each other respect and seeing one another as valuable doesn't take the strength of Mother Theresa. But emotional intimacy, vulnerability, humility, and deep sharing—the ingredients of true *knowing—those* things don't come easy.

The broken and wounded parts of ourselves burrow down deep and beg to be hidden. It takes every ounce of courage in us to truly open up and share at a heart level with other people. Most people are too scared to emotionally join their partners, to *know* them on a vulnerable level. *Truly knowing* your partner requires you to risk feeling shameful, embarrassed, and weak. It requires pushing through your fears of being exposed as flawed and needy. It is hard to admit that we cannot exist as self-sufficient people, and that we have needs that only relationship with other people can fill. This is hard, necessary work—the kind of work that Rebecca and Tim could not, or would not, do.

Turning Losers into Lovers

You may be familiar with Losers in your workplace or friendship circles. Take Tina, for instance. You recently went to a Christmas party and saw Tina near the refreshments. You and Tina have talked before; in fact, your sons played on the same sports teams. You walk over to her and begin talking. You get the feeling that she is looking through you, like as if she is feigning interest. Soon, you see her scan the room and make a friendly gesture toward someone else. She breaks away from you, and you feel wounded. Tina is your *Loser*. Tina may be a very nice person. She probably respects you as a person, but she just doesn't want to take the time to get to know you. She may not be snobby, or rude, or any other negative thing your wounded ego would like to make up about her. However, she will lose out on getting to know you.

I, myself, am acquainted with Losers, and have been one too. As a child, I moved often, changing schools sometimes twice a year. I was forever the new girl. I learned to adapt, to make new friends, and to invite myself into firmly established groups. I learned how to be brave in almost any social circumstance. From these experiences, I gained a sense of adventure. I experienced many new places and people, and I got was good at trying new things. One thing I lacked, however, was history. History is built by shared experiences over time. Few got the chance to really *know* me. I rarely got the chance to make myself known or work out difficulties with a friend, because

I didn't stay long enough to have difficulties. Without this sense of history and roots, I didn't get to know my friends well. I learned to keep things superficial and light.

As an adult, I made the friends in my life Losers as a defense mechanism against the pain that would be coming if we eventually said goodbye. To overcome this Loser pattern, I worked hard to open up, to choose safe people with whom I could be vulnerable, and to face conflict instead of avoiding it. I've learned that it's okay to form roots, to allow myself to be known deeply, to be vulnerable with friends, to work through differences without saying goodbye, and to make history with others. I've learned to turn the Losers, including myself, into the Lucky Ones. And you can too.

Have you considered that you may be someone else's personal Loser? Are there people in your life that you see but have no interest in knowing? Or maybe you made a friend a Loser by keeping her at arm's length. What about with your partner? Do you shy away from difficult conversations because of how vulnerable they make you feel? You don't have to. You don't have to push off others to avoid true intimacy. Similarly, you don't have to try so hard to make a Loser love you. If you keep reading, you will learn how to relate to them in a positive and healthy way, and maybe even turn them into Lovers.

Qualities and Characteristics of Losers

- They avoid your attempts at sharing personal feelings, thoughts, or ideas.
- They are not fully committed to self-improvement or personal growth.
- They allow you to share deeply with them but don't return the gift.

- They appear disinterested or unresponsive.
- They act annoyed with you when you have feelings.
- They may say things like, "You shouldn't feel that way," or "Why do you always make a big deal out of small issues," or "You should get over it," or "Stop asking me how I feel," or "I'm just not an emotional person. You're expecting too much from me."
- They seem nice and cordial, but they're closed off and private.
- They give the bare minimum of what you ask.
- You feel like they hide their true feelings about you.
- They are unexpressive when it comes to words of affirmation.
- Emotional intimacy scares them.
- Growing into a functioning adult scares them.
- They meet your vulnerabilities with indifference, silence, or with ways to fix your problem.

How Does it Feel to Be with a Loser?

- **Hopeless.** Sometimes you feel like you are trying to draw water from an empty well. You feel like you're the only adult in the relationship who is trying to hold the family together.
- **Dismissed.** You feel unimportant and not taken seriously.
- **Unimportant.** You feel that your partner's emotional withdrawal is silent rejection or disinterest.
- **Unreachable.** Whether you and your partner lack the skills to connect, or your partner withholds affection and connection, you feel inaccessible.
- **Abandoned and Alone.** You feel like the person who is supposed to love you the most rejects you at your core. You feel like your partner is either unable or unwilling to emotionally connect with you, leaving your heart empty.

- **Too Much**. You feel like you must just be too much to handle: too needy, too sensitive, and too emotional.

- **Cut off.** You feel cut off from your own true feelings. Your authentic needs, wants, and feelings remain unknown and unmet, like exposed nerves at the skin's surface. Because the pain of rejection is so pronounced, you decide to make the needs disappear.

- **Hopelessly Numb.** Once the pain of loneliness settles in, you lose hope that the relationship will ever improve. Your attempts at connecting result in standoffs and blowups, and the relationship worsens. You resign yourself to go through the motions. It's easier to not feel. The feelings and needs get buried deeper.

- **Guilty.** Your buried need to be known goes underground where it gains in power. Since the need has already been labeled unacceptable, it finds unacceptable means for satiation, (i.e., flirting with a coworker, reading or watching erotica, extramarital affairs.) You have guilt for experiencing the intense emotional and physical arousal. But once the feelings erupt from their burial ground, you can't seem to turn them off.

Why You Are Attracted to Losers

If you feel trapped in a cycle of wanting love from a Loser but never getting it, chances are you have a significant Loser in your past. You may have had good parents who loved you, but that relationship only went so far. Maybe your needs were met, but you never felt known, affirmed, or liked. You never felt drawn out, sought after, pursued, and worthy of your parent's full attention.

In fact, "Knowing Tasks" of parenting are often the first things to go in a busy or stressful family environment. "Knowing Tasks" include taking the time to pursue the child's heart, fears, insecurities, and dreams. Knowing a child takes a lot of time, concerted effort, and patience. It also takes a parent who knows and is comfortable with him or herself too.

If a parent is depressed, works too much, is barely surviving, or is emotionally detached in any way, there is no energy left for the hard task of *knowing* the child. When parents are not emotionally in tune with their own needs and unable to meet those needs in healthy ways, they will be unable to meet the needs of their children. Oftentimes, people treat their emotional needs through dysfunctional means such as love and sex addictions, alcohol and drug addictions, controlling behaviors, rage, and codependency. Real and legitimate needs go unmet and retreat underground. Parents in pain inevitably cause pain to their children. Parents lay down a pattern of mistreating needs and emotional pain, and inevitably their children learn to do the same.

For example, if a child's need for comfort arises and is consistently met with the parent's preoccupation, then the child's need is unrecognized and goes underground. The need becomes a vacuum. When the child grows to adulthood, she will likely seek comfort from sources who will reinforce her negative pattern. In other words, she'll keep looking for the same preoccupied type of person to fill the original hole created in childhood. She does this unconsciously, but the power of that vacuum is fierce, attracting all kinds of people and things that cannot truly meet her need for comfort. She will reenact the pattern of the past by finding similar people to reinforce the hole.

Backstory

Remember Rebecca and Tim's story from the beginning of the chapter? Rebecca grew up with parents who showed sufficient provision, guidance, and support. They supported her cheerleading activities, provided means for her college, and gave her a foundation of Christian faith. However, Rebecca's parents lived in a cold marriage and were unable to give her the emotional love she needed. While her mother pleaded for her husband's attention with tears, her father exercised control through his punishing silence and withheld affection. Rarely affectionate, Rebecca's father modeled a stoic existence that communicated "expressing feelings is considered weak." A very successful lawyer, he spent many hours at work and his weekends were away on business.

When Rebecca entered adolescence, she began to test the house rules, stay out later than permitted, and wear more makeup. Her mother worried and fretted over Rebecca's safety when she went out, and often Rebecca was met at the door by her crying mother, saying things like, "I'm just so worried about you. Why didn't you call? Don't you care about how you're affecting me?"

Rebecca resented the pressure she felt to take care of her mother's feelings. Rebecca resented the fact that she identified more with her disengaged father. Deep down, she longed for his attention and approval, but felt weak admitting it. Being weak meant being like her mother, and she vowed never to be like her. Her unmet needs drove her to early sexual activity with older boys. By age 14, she was sexually active. Rebecca felt guilty about this, but her uncontrollable desire to feel loved won out.

Rebecca left home for college with a Soul Hole—an unmet need to be known deeply. Her father was too absent, too disinterested, and too preoccupied to seek and pursue his daughter. Rebecca's father, closed off from his own emotions, was unable to truly know and join with Rebecca. Rebecca's mother abandoned her role as the responsible adult, and Rebecca took over the care of her mother's overly prominent emotional needs.

When Rebecca was with Tim, she felt something very familiar and comfortable. And no wonder, the dynamic between them was the same between her and her father. She was familiar coming in second place to her father's work. She was familiar with saying to herself, "I don't want to be a bother." She would soon become familiar with coming in second to Tim's mother. This would be her role. She postured herself as self-sufficient, independent, and strong, so that Tim would never have cause to leave her. She was afraid of being perceived as weak, like her mother, so she refused to make her personal needs important. It was much safer to have no needs at all. Being in a Loser relationship was all she knew. Unwittingly, she kept the cycle going so she would never be abandoned by Tim. Little did she know, she was already abandoning herself.

Why You Stay

If you are resonating with Rebecca, or could easily put yourself in her shoes, then ask yourself this question, "What is my payoff for keeping the status quo?"

Most people don't believe they can have better. Some don't want to risk losing what they have so they can gain something better. Most, though, just don't know better exists. Losers can have a certain power over you, a power that you give them, to keep you hooked and hanging on. Ask yourself, "When my heart is ignored, why do I keep going back for more?" The answer is that you've been conditioned to *expect* to be ignored. You've been conditioned from an early age that being *known* is just not for you. Maybe you're not worth it, or maybe you yearn for something that doesn't exist. Whatever it is, you don't know how to get it, so you just stay stuck with what you have. You think being known and being loved cannot happen at the same time.

. . . .

You've been conditioned to expect to be ignored.

. . . .

There is a reason people stay in unhealthy patterns. What is your payoff for keeping things as they are? The answer to this question is the key to understanding your deepest fear. Ultimately, if you are afraid of being alone, abandoned, controlled, or manipulated, you will do anything to keep that from happening. Maybe your payoff is remaining aloof so you don't have to appear weak. Maybe it is putting up with a cold marriage so you won't be alone. If you have shame over being exposed as flawed or weak, then being with a Loser is a perfect fit. He will never require you to open up to him, exposing your vulnerabilities. Or maybe your payoff is looking and feeling like the "good wife," never asking too much from your partner.

. . . .

What is your payoff for keeping things as they are?
The answer to this question is the key to
understanding your deepest fear.

. . . .

Here are some questions to consider:
- Are you afraid of being thought of as weak, dumb, inadequate, or foolish?

- Are you worried that if you show your authentic self, you will be rejected, so you stay guarded?
- Are you afraid of being alone and abandoned?
- Do you believe that if you are vulnerable with your partner, he will shut down, think you're silly, or become angry?
- Are you afraid that you are just too much, too emotional, or too needy for your partner, and that if he found out just how much you really need, he would think you weren't worth the effort?

Your payoff for keeping status quo costs more than you know. You abandon yourself each time you push your feelings down. You devalue yourself each time you tell yourself, "It's okay; my needs aren't important." You lose a piece of yourself with each passing Loser choice.

Chances are your need to be known has gone underground and is being medicated by something you consider taboo, such as a hidden addiction, affair, depression, eating disorder, or rage problem. Unmet needs don't just go away; they go underground. You may be trying to fill your Soul Hole with something or someone else to feel alive, feel control, or numb the pain, and you have found that the excitement is short-lived, the cost is too great, and the pain just comes back. It doesn't have to be this way.

Ryan and Jessica's Story

Ryan and Jessica had been married eight years when Jessica found unexplained charges on their credit card statement. After investigating the charges and their source, she was shocked to find out her husband was paying for online pornography. This hurt Jessica deeply and brought up feelings of betrayal and self-doubt. She confronted Ryan and he became defensive. The more defensive he got, the more hopeless she felt.

Jessica's feelings of rejection seemed overwhelming. She felt small and insignificant and all alone in the world. How could he do this to her, and why wouldn't he acknowledge that his actions hurt her?

Jessica recalled the summer when her family fell apart. She was twelve and her mother and father had been fighting a lot. Her father had been caught having an affair with a woman while he was away on business trips. This woman worked with him, and Jessica had met her at company picnics. She was tall, blond, and curvy. In Jessica's twelve-year-old mind, she thought this woman must be the ideal woman. She could tell that all the men looked at her, and she must like it.

That summer, Jessica's mother broke down and became emotionally unavailable to her children. She stayed in her room. She didn't make dinner. She didn't go out. Jessica felt as if she had lost her mother and her father that summer. She started to hate that other woman. Jessica's parents stayed married, but she remembers the family never being the same after that. They didn't take family vacations, Mom seemed depressed all the time, and Dad worked a lot. Jessica's mother and father were so preoccupied with their own issues that Jessica was forgotten.

When she confronted Ryan with her discovery, all those old feelings of despair and betrayal and anger came flooding back. It was hours before Ryan talked to her again. But when he did, he came with tears in his eyes. He confessed he had been viewing pornography on his laptop, and he was trying to hide it from her. He told her he was ashamed of himself, and he was sorry for hurting her. He said he felt a relief that she knew because now maybe he could finally quit. He said he knew it was wrong, but it became a bad habit that he couldn't break, and he wanted to be rid of it.

Ryan's humble confession surprised Jessica. She didn't know how to respond to him. This wasn't in the script of her parents' playbook. She had never experienced a humble confession before. She never heard her dad say he was sorry. She never saw her mother recover from the betrayal. She never felt worth the acknowledgement and the apology. But here it was.

Jessica sobbed with Ryan. She was still hurt deeply by Ryan's actions, but the hurt was mixed with relief that he was honest. She felt closer to him than before. They went to couples counseling, Ryan started going to a men's accountability group, and Jessica began the long road to forgiveness. Jessica learned to be open with Ryan about her fears and body image insecurities. She felt exposed and vulnerable during these conversations, but was met with Ryan's genuine understanding and willingness to empathize. He shared with her the growing competitiveness at work and how he feels inadequate.

During counseling, Ryan discovered the significance of his mother's words to him as a boy. Ryan's mother shamed him with emasculating pet names, and implied he was dirty for having sexual feelings. Ryan needed to learn that his sexuality was clean and good and healthy, and that his masculinity was not dependent on his mother's opinion. When Jessica heard Ryan share these things, and how it hurt him as a child, she could see that his pornography use was not about her. This helped in the forgiveness process.

Ryan and Jessica turned what could have been a deal breaker for their marriage into an opportunity to draw closer. They pushed past their fears of sharing emotionally intimate memories and the insecurities that had crippled them before, and clung to each other for healing. Their story is an example of how true healing can occur in the context of the marriage relationship.

These are core fears locked deep inside that come naturally and habitually. These fears, once useful in keeping us safe and okay in childhood, are no longer useful in forming healthy adult relationships. Our happiness and relational health depend on us pushing past these fears to connect vulnerably and authentically with the people we love. By pushing past these useless fears, we can begin to "Live in the Pink" (more on this later) with the significant people in our lives.

The following diagram describes the secret motives and fears of each person in Loser Relationships compared to what is considered healthy relating. You can see how fear, idolatry, avoidance, denial, and shame result in broken relationships. However, love, intimacy, and grace result in a deep sense of acceptance and attachment. This diagram is helpful in recognizing your own motivations and how misguided motivations can result in the opposite of what you want.

The Loser, Over-Functioner, and Healthy Paradigms[9]

Loser Paradigm	Over-Functioner	Healthy Paradigm
Fear—I fear getting so close to someone that they could use or control me.	***Fear***—I fear being controlled by his silence and detachment.	***Love***—Love casts out all fear. There is no fear in love.
Idolatry—I want other people to like me. I worship the good opinion of others.	***Idolatry***—I trust myself to keep me safe and loved, not God.	***True Worship***—I seek to surrender my fears and weaknesses to God.
Avoidance—I avoid conflict, intimacy, and vulnerability in order to keep myself safe.	***Controlling***—I feel vulnerable when I'm not in control.	***Embrace Intimacy Opportunities***—Because I am safely held and unconditionally loved by God, I can attach to others without fear or dimishment of my own strength.
Distraction Tactics—I use joking, excuses, devices, work, or physical tiredness to avoid conflict, intimacy, and vulnerability.	***Complaint and Blame Tactics***—I pick fights just to feel something other than the "nothing" that's between us.	
Denial—I won't admit that I need intimacy with others.	***Denial***—That I have anything to do with the intimacy problem in this marriage.	***Reality***—I have an accurate assessment of myself and others, and am able to admit weaknesses without shame.
Shame—Intimacy makes me feel inadequate, so I avoid the things that lead to intimacy.	***Shame***—Vulnerability makes me feel weak and needy, so I maintain power and control in order not to feel shame associated with weakness.	***Grace***—I have unmerited favor and can live an open life of trust and love.
Abandonment—I value being safe from shame more than seeking intimacy with my partner, resulting in feelings of loneliness.	***Abandonment***—I push my partner further away with my controlling compliants and blame, and end up feeling abandoned.	***Belonging***—Because I believe God cannot abandon me, I will not abandon myself. I can find intimacy with God and others without fear of being controlled.

---

9 Idolatry used here means to worship someone or something other than God. When we honor God above others, then we agree with God's natural order of things. We see people as equals, not greater or less than ourselves. We have reasonable expectations of others and ourselves, and see God as a Source of life instead of others.

Steps to Living in the Pink

"Living in the Pink" is a phrase meaning "in excellent condition," and "at the pinnacle of health, happiness, and fulfillment." The following Relationship REPS are your keys to Living in the Pink.

R Restore Order through Boundaries

When you think of boundaries, saying "no" to others may come to mind first. However, saying "no" to yourself is also necessary. You may have a good idea of how to say "no" to yourself regarding typical temptations like overindulging or gossiping or yelling. But what about the deeper things that take a little more insight?

When couples get close to the vulnerable edge of intimacy, they often become afraid and defensive. Couples in Loser relationships take turns fending off getting too close, too vulnerable, and too exposed.

Losers can often feel inadequate when their partner expresses emotion or asks for more heartfelt communication. Not knowing what to do, how to connect, or how to make their partner's tears stop, their threatened system enacts flight or fight responses. They feel threatened by what they don't understand or can't fix, and therefore either underreact (dismiss or ignore) or overreact (yell and blame). They develop defense mechanisms to protect themselves from the shame of feeling inadequate, the fear of being seen as weak, and the perceived humiliation of being "less than." Defense mechanisms are used to protect but unfortunately result in decreased intimacy with the self and with others. These mechanisms distract us from knowing the self and others. Some common unhealthy Defense Mechanisms are:

- *Intellectualization:* an overemphasis on thinking when faced with unacceptable or overwhelming emotions. You express sadness that you were just laid off at work, and your partner says, "Statistically, 1 out of 4 people will be laid off in their lifetime."

- *Blame Shifting:* resistant or refusing to admit wrongdoing and diverting the conversation to the partner's faults. You tell your partner that you are afraid that he's spending too much time at work and missing out on your kids' lives. Your partner responds with, "Oh, you're one to talk. You call quality time with the kids letting them watch videos all day?"

- *Archeological Digging:* bringing past mistakes into the present conversation to deflect responsibility or intimacy. You and your partner disagree about the appropriate amount to pay your kids for allowance. One of you says, "You're always trying to spend us into a hole! Remember when you racked up our credit cards last year? Here you go again!"

- *Regression:* reacting to unwanted thoughts, feelings, or actions with immature, childlike behaviors (i.e., tantrums, sulking, paybacks, silence treatment, impulsivity, hostility, lashing or acting out). Your forty-five-year-old partner dissolves into an emotional wreck when faced with his own failures and flaws.

- *Projection:* misattribution of unwanted thoughts, feelings, or actions onto another person. For example, you are deathly afraid of being out of control, so you blame your partner for being too controlling.

- *Fort Building:* defensiveness that results in two sides or two enemies, to avoid humbleness and intimacy. When asked by your partner if you could clean the house more often, you become defensive and say, "I can't believe you have the nerve to ask me that. I do the best I can, no thanks to you!"

Restoring the boundaries in your emotional world should include noticing these Defense Mechanisms and employing ways to step through them. Say "no" to defending yourself and "yes" to opening yourself up.

E Experience God

Partners of Losers must give up expectations to be heard or affirmed perfectly. You don't need to be heard or affirmed perfectly by your Loser because you are able to receive that from God. Your need to be affirmed all the time and perfectly can only be done by the perfect Friend and Father, God. Your partner can never fill the hole that God is supposed to fill. What is needed to experience this affirmation is regular healthy self-talk to remind you of the unconditional love God has for you. This will help you hold on to yourself while you share with your partner.

Holding on to yourself, while sharing vulnerably with your partner, sounds like this in your head: "I just told him about an important need. I feel exposed and raw. But I'm not alone. I'm not weak just because I have a weakness. I am strong in God's strength. I am not needy just because I have needs. I am blessed abundantly beyond measure. I am okay and will be okay. Even when exposing weakness, flaws, and needs, I am okay." You can be this confident, inside and out, when you:

- First, commit to God, the Good Parent, that you will pay attention to your own needs. Commit to revealing yourself fully to Him with all your human motivations—the good, the desperate, and the ugly. Ask Him to reveal the hidden parts of your heart to you and to make known your needs, hopes, desires, and wounds. Specifically, ask Him to reveal the areas of shame locked inside you that need His comfort.

- Second, actively participate in the meeting of your own needs. Don't just pray about it, think about it, or talk about it. Behave in a way that recognizes and affirms your needs. Practice good self-care. Practice loving boundaries. Talk lovingly to yourself. Offer yourself forgiveness for being an imperfect human. This is the transformative evidence of God in your life.

- Thirdly, look to God for the meeting of your needs. Sometimes we look to our partners to fulfill needs and expectations that they humanly are unable to fulfill. When we receive God's abundant care and unconditional love, we become less dependent upon flawed human care and love. This concept materializes once you are able to say to God and self, "I will be okay with or without my partner's love because I am found, protected, and supported by God's love first. All other love is bonus."

P Provide Yourself with People

You will need to practice assertiveness in your various social circles: work, church, school, and supportive groups. These people will be a testing ground for you to practice valuing yourself. Your needs, hopes, and desires are important. Stop acting as though they are not. Write them down. This practice is healthy, not selfish. When you admit that your needs, hopes, and desires are important, you free yourself to creatively brainstorm ways to meet them. Prioritizing yourself is you showing up to your life. Speaking your mind is embracing the voice God gave you.

God has given and will give you people, situations, and relationships with which to practice assertiveness skills. Try not to shy away from these opportunities; instead, embrace them. Instead of avoiding conflict, lean into relationships with people. Instead of ignoring awkward silences or snappy words, ask questions about them with the purpose of problem solving and bonding.

Asserting your needs is not yelling, shouting, cussing, or pouting. Asserting yourself is stating, expressing, maintaining, and putting into action. When trying to schedule a work meeting, recognize your schedule constraints as much as you value others' schedules. When coordinating car pool, recognize your needs as much as the other moms' needs. When your needs are not being taken into consideration, you should speak your mind about what you want. When talking with your husband, remember to value your needs as much as you value his.

A sign that hangs in my office reads,

"I'll not shut up or blow up.
I'll show up, and stand my sacred ground."

We can easily under- or overreact because of fear and shame, but we don't have to have these reactions. We can merely show up, show ourselves, and make ourselves known. We have the power to know ourselves, to affirm ourselves, and show others who we are too. Our sacred ground is the foundation of love that God has given each of us to stand on. Each of us is valuable, innately worth respect and dignity. When we embrace our true identity, value, and purpose through Christ, we can be who we really are—shameless, strong, free people who light up the world.

One day, at a resale shop, I picked up a pair of jeans with no price tag attached. I tried them on, liked them, and carried them up to the counter for purchase. I brought up another similar pair as a price comparison to help the salesclerk out. When she couldn't find a price tag, she looked through her computer system. While she struggled to come up with a price, I presented the comparison jeans. She then said she would charge me $25—$5 more than the comparison pair with the tag. I decided this would be a good time to practice my assertiveness skills. I told her I wanted to pay $20 for them, not $25. She gave me a few reasons why she thought my pair were worth more than the comparison pair. I just kindly (with a smile, of course!) stated that I wanted to pay $20 for them, and that I thought that was a fair price. She agreed and sent me on my way (glad to get me out of her hair, no doubt!). This assertiveness exercise was not about winning an argument or fighting for justice. It was about expressing what I wanted and not being ashamed or afraid of wanting something. You can do it, too.

God will supply you with the people and situations you need to practice your new assertiveness skills.

When you show up asserting your needs, hopes, and desires, you may or may not be received the way you expect. It doesn't matter. Stay loving, respectful, and grounded in God's love. Relationship change takes concerted, repetitive effort. You must build your underutilized assertiveness muscles in yourself, and your relationship must make incremental allowances to adjust to you. Give this process time and prayer.

Living in the Pink does not come overnight. It is a sustained challenge that requires patience, forgiveness, denial of instant gratification, character reformation, and lots of love. Learn to laugh at yourself. Learn to give it to God faster. Learn to have patience with yourself and others.

Relational health will come. Unconditional love will be offered. True intimacy is available. Offer it first to yourself, and then invite it from others. With some patience, practice, and intentional intimacy, someday you will be able to look at your Loser and say, "You are now my Lover," and mean it.

S Seek Intimacy

Colleen was in a pickle. Married for eighteen years, she and her husband, Eric, were stuck. Both were in church ministry, committed to each other through thick and thin, and parents of three daughters. But Colleen and Eric were getting on each other's nerves. The familiar fights, unresolved issues, and dysfunctional patterns that once were tolerable were now major stumbling blocks. They agreed on the big stuff—purpose, values, parenting, and finances—but there were days Colleen felt like they were a complete emotional mismatch. "Sometimes I doubt I can live with this emotional caveman for another twenty years. He just doesn't get my heart. He's so concerned with analyzing the argument, he completely misses ME!"

They had just been through twelve weeks of marital counseling and took a break because they didn't seem to get anywhere. The long and short of it was that he was too much in his head, and she was too much in her heart. He intellectualized most of their arguments, while she emotionally collapsed in the middle of them.

. . . .

They committed to love each other till death did them part, but sometimes wished that death would come sooner rather than later!

. . . .

She asked, "What is wrong with us? I feel like we are loving, mature, Christian people. So why can't we figure this marriage thing out? It feels like other couples figure it out. What is wrong with us?"

"Nothing is wrong with you or your marriage, Colleen," I said. "You are going to a deeper level of intimacy than you have been before. It's uncharted territory. You are both resisting the vulnerability and power of its pull. Some couples give up at this point, because it requires so much humility. But stay with it! This is an opportunity of a lifetime!"

Losers are afraid of intimacy. Intimacy requires you to be seen completely and to be known deeply. It also requires great risk. There is no greater risk than sharing your heart with no guarantee that you'll get it back. Eric hid from vulnerability behind his intellectualism, and Colleen hid from her power behind her tears. Emotional intimacy is not for the fainthearted. Colleen and Eric's marriage needed more from them than they had given so far. In key emotional parts of their lives, they still acted like Losers. They were afraid that deeper intimacy would reveal deeper flaws, deeper weaknesses, and wounds from shame felt long ago. Familiar patterns of avoiding conflict, self-righteous intellectualizing, and childish attempts at shifting blame would be cauterized once and for all. Healing, freedom, and love await the victors on the other side of the chasm, and it takes trust and humility to get there.

Practice Intentional Vulnerability

Since Losers *see* you, but don't *know* you, you will have to take the first step in making yourself known. Take a risk and share your feelings without melting down. Hold on to yourself, and let God hold you while you take the necessary risk of sharing from your heart. Teach your partner how to respond, what you need, and how you need it.

It is not the Loser's job to draw you out. It is your job to show up. Losers are largely out of touch with their own needs, so they won't naturally know how to tune into yours. You must make the first move in sharing your true self, your true feelings. Be careful not to use this time of sharing to point fingers, attack, or blame. Use this time to share your thoughts, feelings, and needs.

Lean into Intimacy

Here is an example dialogue from Eric and Colleen:

Colleen: When I tell you how I feel, and start crying because it hurts so much, you start analyzing our fight. You start talking about "why" you say things, and "why" I feel the way I do. All I want is for you to feel *with* me in the moment.

Eric: What do you mean, feel *with* you in the moment? I do feel with you!

Colleen: No, I know you have feelings. I'm not saying that you don't. What I want is for you to stop analyzing "why" I feel the way I do, and just *feel* with me.

Eric: (blank stare)

Colleen: Okay, let me show you. I feel alone, hopelessly alone in life when you ignore my tears and launch into psychoanalysis. I don't want you to figure me out or us out; I just want you to look in my eyes, touch me, and say something like, "I know. I get what you're saying. Feeling lonely is scary."

Eric: But I feel like you are blaming me for making you feel lonely—like it's all my fault. When you blame me, I don't feel like showing compassion!

Colleen: Okay, I understand. I will watch how I say things so I don't use blaming language. But, if I use "I feel lonely when you x,y,z" that is not an attack or blaming. That is me just telling you what I'm feeling.

Eric: Okay, I can get that. When you say, "I feel lonely when you psychoanalyze us," I won't get defensive as if you're blaming me for all our problems.

Colleen: Yeah, totally, because I'm not. I know we are both to blame for our problems. I just want you to hurt *with* me. That you get me. That you understand me. That you're *with* me. As long as I know that you and I are in this marriage together, then I stop feeling so alone. When you hurt with me, I stop feeling alone. But when I'm crying, and you are somewhere in your head explaining me away, I feel totally lost.

Eric: Okay. I do hurt with you. I don't want you to feel alone. It's definitely easier explaining things than it is sitting and watching you cry. Then I feel like you're blaming me for your pain, and I get mad.

Colleen: Yeah, your anger really makes me feel alone too. But I don't want to start another fight, so let's talk about that later. I feel like we are getting somewhere now. I'm not asking you to sit and *watch* me cry. Just put your hand on my knee. Just comfort me. Just listen without saying anything.

Eric: Okay, I think I understand. When I see you cry, I will reach out to touch you instead of trying to explain things. I'll try to hear your heart instead of trying to tell you what's in my head.

Colleen: Yes, sweetie, that would mean so much to me. I am interested in hearing what's in your head too! You often see the dynamic between us so clearly. I just need to know you hear my heart first.

Eric: And you will stop using blaming language like somehow I'm *trying* to hurt you, right?

Colleen: Yes, I will watch my words. I know you love me. I will stop using blaming language.

Colleen shared from her deepest fear of abandonment. She made herself extremely vulnerable by sharing her experience of feeling "hopelessly alone." The abandoned and alone feeling is difficult to admit to yourself, let alone to admit to your partner. If Eric would have rejected, judged, or dismissed her during this conversation, their marriage would have been in a precarious place. Colleen bravely told Eric what she needed in great detail and with attention to specifics (i.e., touch my knee, just listen without saying anything, say "I understand," or "tell me more so I can understand"), and Eric responded with care and humility. Instead of building walls, Eric went deeper into vulnerability with Colleen, and Colleen bonded. Colleen and Eric triumphed, reaching deeper intimacy than they had ever reached before.

The fears that cause Losers to miss out on truly knowing one another are not stronger than love. The bible says, "There is no fear in love. But perfect love drives out fear…"[10] Let the work of love, intimacy, and true knowing change you and your relationships for good. Loser relationships have a great potential for maturing, deepening, and growing.

Losers can become lovers; in fact, deep down, Losers really want loving intimacy—to know and be known. But that is not true of all people. In this next chapter, you will learn about a very different type of partner—a partner who already knows you. In fact, he believes he knows you better than you know yourself. This type of partner has

---

10 1 Jn 4:18 (New International Version).

the capacity to drain the life right out of your veins without you even realizing he's sunk his teeth in you. He is the User.

Chapter 5

USERS: There's Only Enough Love Here for One of Us

"How starved you must have been that my heart became a meal for your ego."

—Amanda Torroni

"I don't care what you think unless it is about me."

—Kurt Cobain

"God opposes the proud but gives grace to the humble." [11]

My breath puffed into the crisp autumn air like billows of smoke, and I was struck with the vibrant colors of fall. The changing leaves hung against the clear blue sky like rubies. As I walked from my car to my office door, I mentally ran through my schedule for the day. It would be a relatively light day, with just a few clients. I would use the extra time for billing and writing. Maybe I could leave early today and enjoy the outdoors by walking my dog. Lord knows, he's much better behaved after a walk! Once I entered my office, I glanced out my window and saw a man taking pictures of

---

11   1 Pt 5:5 (New International Version).

the colorful trees in the office parking lot. I looked closer at the man and was immediately overtaken with dread. The hair on the back of my neck stood up, and I gulped hard. What was *he* doing here? I felt an invasion of my personal space. The man was hundreds of feet away, separated by bricks and glass, but I felt as though he was breathing down my neck. He looked up at my office window and smiled. I stepped away from the window, turned down the blinds, and breathed a prayer.

He had been a client, or, rather, the *husband* of a client. Helena was a thirty-year-old mother of two, delightful and bubbly, who came to counseling for help with her marriage to Scott. Helena seemed to always be smiling, even when she talked about her problems, and her problems were sizable. Her husband Scott was the pastor of a church and well-loved by everyone. His charisma, knowledge of scripture, and charming personality kept him in high regards with their church and denomination leadership. But Helena rarely saw the charming side of her husband at home.

It seemed like Scott tolerated her for the most part but sometimes she felt he downright hated her. She blamed his curt answers and harsh tone on work stress and tried to give him more space, more forgiveness, and more grace. She thought to herself, "I should do what I can to make his life easier. Maybe then he'll be happy with me." She pitched in at church when a volunteer was a no-show. She ran the children's ministry after the Children's Director left for another church. She kept her house clean and her kids quiet when her husband got home—all with eagerness to please him. But pleasing the unpleasable was an impossible job.

She read books on marriage about the differences between men and women, about how to communicate effectively with a man, and what men need to feel respected. She changed the way she talked to him. She gave herself to him fully. She asked him what she could do to win his affections back. His responses to her loving attempts were critiques about her personality, judgments about her motives, and vague complaints about her roles as mother and wife. She couldn't quite nail down what exactly she was supposed to do to make him happy.

Over time, she decided she could live in a loveless marriage because Scott was so good and godly toward everyone else. She watched how he attended the sick in the hospital, the way he raised funds for the women's shelter, and how he dropped everything on his calendar to meet with a church member in need.

Helena kept a smile on her face while she was telling me the details of her previous year of marriage. I questioned her about this, to which she replied with a smile, "If I stop smiling, I may completely drown." And then she told me the worst of it.

"Two weeks ago, while Scott was in the shower, someone texted him. I looked to see if it was important—you know, to decide whether I should interrupt him or not. Scott hates missing important calls. It was from a preschool teacher at church. I investigated further and found this wasn't the first time she had texted him. I wondered what she needed, thinking it was odd that she didn't call me first if it concerned our children. I investigated further and found that this wasn't the first time she had texted him. I found more than I ever wanted to know." Helena's simple smile finally turned down, and she began to weep. Through heavy sobs, Helena confirmed what I already suspected—Scott was deeply involved with another woman.

The next few months revealed more sordid details of Scott's dishonesty, his manipulation of the truth, and his growing contempt for Helena. He denied having any relationship with the other woman beyond "pastoral counseling." Scott admitted that he'd met with her several times to help her through her own divorce, and maybe he shouldn't have met with her outside of the office, but the texts were completely innocent, and there was nothing to worry about. In fact, Scott felt outraged at Helena's distrust, her fanatical jealousy, and her digging into other people's confidential texts! His parishioners rely on him to maintain their confidentiality! How could she betray their trust like that?

Helena went silent. Although she didn't think he was right, she agreed to let it go. It was much easier to just let him win. Scott then talked about his work stress, that his associate pastor and he weren't seeing eye to eye, and that the pressures of work were extreme. He shared with her about how hard he had been working for the Lord and for the church, and that it never seemed like enough. With tears he said, "Helena, sometimes I'm just so overwhelmed with God's work, I just don't know what to do. And you! You just keep pressuring me, hounding me! I can't just relax in my own home!"

Desperate to feel loved and needed, she overlooked the warning signs. Glad that her husband was finally opening up to her, she hugged him and promised to help lessen his workload. She wouldn't question his texts anymore and would give him the benefit of the doubt. Maybe that is what loving wives do—let things go and overlook the bad. She was conflicted between what she knew in her head and the need to be loved in her heart. What was she supposed to believe? What was she supposed to do? How was she supposed to feel?

Helena knew there would be consequences for standing up for herself and her needs. She knew Scott would punish her with the silent treatment, label her a crazy jealous wife, or maybe even turn the kids away from her. Though she was not fully conscious of these very real consequences, she had a deep knowledge of her husband's emotionally violent capabilities. Accepting Scott's behaviors without condition was certainly the path of least resistance. The safer path.

One day, unannounced, Scott arrived with Helena at my office for her scheduled appointment. Helena tried to hide her agitation with her usual happy expression and said, "I hope you don't mind, but Scott really wanted to come along today." I could see the hope in her eyes, and while I usually don't accept last minute surprises like this, I wanted to hope right alongside Helena.

I replied, "Scott, you are welcome to join us in counseling today, because Helena requests it, but just this one time. Couples counseling would need to be done with a marriage therapist, separate from Helena's sessions." I asked what precisely they hoped to accomplish today by meeting together.

Without pause, Scott smiled and said, "Helena has been so upset lately; I just want to be here to show her support. She's said so much about you, and I wanted to meet you for myself so I can know how to help her." Scott was pressed, shaven, and smelling like the fragrance inserts in a *GQ* magazine. He flashed a wide grin my way and complimented my antique curio cabinet. "I'd guess that it is not from around here. I have an eye for fine valuables and antiques." He was right. The cabinet was from France.

"You have been so helpful to Helena. I'm glad that she finally has someone she can talk with about her issues." I felt like I was being buttered up—to be eaten. "I don't know if she's told you, but I'm a certified communication specialist. You've probably heard of the Win-Win Communication program?"

"No, I haven't," I replied.

"Oh, all the corporate professionals use it. I would think someone in your profession would know about it. Anyway, I *teach* communication now. Helena has come to some of my classes. We use Win-Win Communication every time we have a conflict. No offense, but I'm not sure there is anything you can teach me we don't already know."

Helena sat by her husband, with a pleasant look. The word "dutiful" came to mind. "Helena, I didn't know you both were so skilled at communication," I said.

With hesitation Helena said, "Yes, I have learned a lot about communication from Scott."

"Tell me again why you both are here. I'm not sure what you are expecting out of today's session," I queried again.

Helena spoke up this time. She bravely ventured out and said, "Well, I'm having trouble moving on from the texts I found between Scott and the church preschool teacher. I'm having trouble with my jealousy."

Scott's smile faltered ever so slightly, but his gaze never flinched. He kept his eye trained on me like a lion on its prey. "That's something she hasn't been able to move past yet." Putting a hand on Helena's knee, he went on, "I think it's because she feels insecure about her weight. She compares herself to other women in the church. I feel bad for her. Maybe you can help her."

I cringed at Scott's disingenuous gesture.

Helena tightened, then straightened, and looked at me squarely. "I'm having trouble moving on from the relationship Scott had with her, because I believe that the relationship is still going on!"

Then Scott slumped, rolled his eyes, and heaved, "Seriously, Helena? Are we going to keep rehashing this? I did not come here to do this! You brought me here to gang up on me with your biased counselor who doesn't know the first thing about me. Let me tell you what this is really about. Let me tell you something I'm sure she's neglected to tell you! Helena is jealous of other women because Helena has body issues. She's so insecure all the time. She can't stand it that other attractive women talk to me."

I inserted myself into the flurry of accusations to bring some calm. If there was some calm, maybe, just maybe, there could be some progress. "Scott, let me stop you for just a minute. Would you be willing, just for a minute, to hear Helena talk about her feelings regarding these texts she's talking about? I'm not saying you've done anything wrong here. I just want to see if we can get some traction between the two of you. If we could find some true intimacy, there may be more understanding between you. One way is by focusing on the *feelings* instead of the accusations. Would you be willing to listen to Helena's feelings for a minute?"

Scott took a deep breath and nodded.

"Helena, would you tell Scott how it makes you feel when you see a text from the preschool teacher?"

Helena quieted herself and then slowly responded, "I feel afraid that I'm not good enough for him. I am afraid that Scott is not the caring man I thought I married. I don't know what else to do to make him happy." I was impressed with Helena's strength to seek intimacy with Scott.

I stayed with Helena for a moment, "So, afraid. You feel afraid that you won't be able to make Scott happy. Is that right?" I went on, "That sounds like a heavy load—to be responsible to make another person happy."

Helena nodded, and I looked at Scott. "Have you felt afraid before, Scott? Afraid that no matter how hard you tried at something, you just weren't going to get it? Do you see how she could feel that same kind of 'afraid?' Are you able to put yourself in her shoes?

I'm just wondering if you could feel what she feels for a minute? About being afraid?"

Scott's expression hardened, "Sure, I understand. She's afraid because she is jealous. She has no reason to accuse me of having an affair. You should see how she is trying to ruin my reputation with her friends at church! I'm the one who is the victim here! The whole church will be reeling if she continues with this lie!"

. . . .

Being responsible for making another person happy is an impossible load.

. . . .

I could see that Scott was becoming upset and didn't have the capacity to connect emotionally with his wife. I was beginning to see that Scott was not a safe person with which to share emotions. It must have taken Helena a good deal of courage to say as much as she did. I know now, what I didn't know at that moment, that Scott was a User who used abusive manipulation and putdowns to deflect blame. Looking back as I write this, it seems silly for me to keep offering Scott another opportunity to connect with Helena, especially when all he did was use those opportunities to blame her. But, I've discovered something about myself in this process too: I am often so shocked by the manipulative cruelty of the User, it takes me a second to catch up to his game. Users are often one step ahead of "us caring types." So, I went on.

"I understand you are upset by all of this, Scott. And understandably so. And I promise to give you a turn in just a minute. But I wonder, could you empathize with Helena? Just see how it might feel to be in her shoes?"

Scott's breathing slowed, and he looked straight at me. "Michelle, has she told you she has an eating disorder? That's what this is all about. She will not address her crazy eating. I believe 'binging and purging' is what you psychologists call it. She will eat bags of potato chips or cookies before I get home from work. Sometimes she'll excuse herself to go to the restroom, but I know what she's doing. Everyone knows that she's barfing her brains out in there. Everyone knows how insecure she is about her weight. She is so obsessed about how fat she is, but she won't do anything about it. She can't stand that other women are in my life. But I am a pastor, and there are going to be women in my life. She just needs to accept that."

I reeled from the harshness of Scott's tone, the brutality of his words, and the searing hatred in his eyes. Not willing to give up on the chance there may be a small window of intervention, I tried to bring Helena back to the conversation by asking, "How do you feel in this moment, Helena? After you shared your feelings, and then heard Scott's reaction, how do you feel right now?"

Helena seemed to be getting smaller and smaller on her side of the couch. Listlessly, she said, "Me? How do I feel right now? Utterly hopeless."

I turned to Scott, hoping to reach him somehow. "What is it like for you to hear that your wife feels utterly hopeless in this marriage?"

Without skipping a beat, like he was commenting on a round of golf, Scott replied, "Like I said, Michelle, she has a lot of issues. I really hope you can help her. That's why I'm here."

What was going on? I felt myself get hot, sweaty, and clammy all at once. I slowed my verbal pace to a dirge, recognizing I was headed toward some invisible battle zone. I said, "Scott, do you realize you just shut your wife down emotionally? You twisted the conversation with such skill and ease, it scares me. Really, I'm terrified. You completely changed the subject and ignored Helena. The tone you used was abusive and cruel." I kept my eyes on his while my heart pounded in my chest. Helena shifted position as if to put distance between her and the battlefield.

"Helena," I concluded. "I don't think we will make any progress on an emotional level between the two of you. In fact, I don't recommend marriage counseling until you, Scott, are committed to your own individual therapy."

Helena saw her opportunity fading and interjected bravely, "Well, since I have this time with both of us together, I have something to say. Scott, I know you are cheating on me. I found text messages and hotel charges on the credit card statement. You can't explain this away anymore. I have given you the benefit of the doubt all this time. And even today, I wasn't going to bring this up unless you refused to listen to me."

"Helena, sweetie, this is what I mean." His porcelain charm began to crack, and he fidgeted. "You spend all this time trying to 'catch me' doing something wrong. There is an obvious explanation for those texts. We've been over this a hundred times. I don't even know what hotel charge you're talking about. You make things up, Helena. You make mountains out of molehills. No husband should have to put up with this! I'm badgered all day long about this stuff!"

Knowing that reaching Scott was hopeless, I turned my attention to helping Helena see the marital dynamic. I asked, "Is this the kind of interaction that usually happens between you two, Helena? You bring a concern to Scott, but he ends up being the victim?"

I landed hard on one of Scott's nerves. Scott's eyes narrowed. "I refuse to sit here any longer and be harangued by you two. You know nothing, Helena! You have no evidence. And you!" Scott glared at me. "Do you have any biblical training at all? Do you have a degree in theology? How do you call yourself a Christian counselor? This isn't *Christian*." The word came out like poison. Then Scott quoted scriptures about Christian devotion, self-sacrifice, and submissiveness. He lectured about his love for his family, and for his church, and how men in his position attract criticism from people who like to throw stones. "I can't believe that churches actually refer their members to you. You are *Mrs.* Hollomon, not *Dr.* Hollomon, right? I may need to tell the pastors in my circle of friends to be more selective in the future."

Helena's face closed, and I could tell she had emotionally left the room. She looked hopeless. I felt sick, and, for the moment, I felt the pain and fear that Helena had been living in for years. To engage Scott at a heart level was futile. To invite Scott to see his own contribution to Helena's pain was pointless. To confront Scott with the truth of his imperfection would bring hostility and revenge. I got a taste of his personal attacks, and it made my stomach turn. The session was over.

Forever. I wanted my safe, tranquil office back. The sleek Scott was a viper under that charming façade. I did my best to maintain professionalism, not giving him any ammo to use against me. "The real issue here is that the state of your marriage is not good. I've witnessed a level of hostility today that is unnerving. This marriage is toxic. Helena, the way Scott talks to you is abusive. Scott, you need serious psychological intervention to learn better ways to treat your wife. And Helena, this marriage is not a safe place for you." Scott was uninterested in what I had to say by this point.

Scott stood up from the couch. "With all due respect, I think we all know that you are out of your league here, *Mrs.* Hollomon.

Our denomination has *doctoral* level pastors and psychologists who are specialists. We won't need your recommendations." He smiled sweetly, and I swear I could smell venom. "No hard feelings, okay?" He reached out to shake my hand.

Helena's smile was gone. In fact, she looked numb. Had something shifted inside her? She said, "I'll call to make an appointment for next week. I'll be coming by myself next time." She moved past Scott without waiting for him. Had she seen the real Scott? Had she finally seen the reality that she was married to a User? That no matter how much grace and space she gave him, no matter how patient of a wife she was, or how many marriage books she read, he would continue to use her for as long as she let him?

Once I closed the door, I was alone with my feelings. What kind of whirlwind had just swept through my office? What kind of unnatural disaster was brewing? I was spent. I sat in my chair and tried to sift through all the various reactions I experienced in working with Scott. Manipulated, embattled, protective, hunted. With slow and heavy breaths, these are the words that came to mind. And frustration—an interminable amount of frustration, as though he were *trying* to frustrate, displace, and seize all plans, intentions, and goals. It was spiritual. It was emotional. His attacks were pointed. All I could think was, "God, help her. She is living a nightmare."

The frustration, exhaustion, and sensory hijack I felt was the aftermath of dealing with a User. This charm-bombing chaos, misinformation, sidetracking, and blaming takes a toll on everyone they get close to, and leaves a path of relational devastation in their wake.

Helena didn't return the next week. She cancelled due to a schedule mix-up. But Scott returned. By himself. He came to my office parking lot to take pictures of the changing leaves. When he looked up into my window and saw me standing there, he smiled and waved as if to say, "I win." Then he left, and I never saw him again.

Helena did return to therapy some weeks later. She eventually found evidence of her husband's *multiple* affairs, refused to keep his secrets for him any longer, and enlisted the help of church leadership. The church board of directors eventually saw through Scott's façade. Scott was put on a leave of absence by his denomination until he successfully completed personal and marital counseling. Though church leadership did what they knew to do, requiring marriage counseling was a complete beat-down for Helena.

First and second attempts at marriage counseling resulted in Scott's effective and calculated manipulation of the facts and refusal to admit any wrongdoing. Scott continued his affair with the other woman. At first, Helena was shocked at how trusting and naïve the marriage counselors were. They seemed to buy everything Scott said, hook, line, and sinker. Helena was angry at how they could be manipulated that way. But then, hadn't she believed Scott all these years? Hadn't she been reluctant to challenge him too? She finally stopped blaming herself for being too weak, too foolish, or too trusting. It wasn't that she was too trusting; wives are supposed to trust their husbands. It was because Scott was *highly skilled* at manipulating people. This was not a naivete problem. This was a character problem—Scott's character.

Scott never finished the prescribed marriage or individual counseling sessions his church leadership required, nor did he ever admit wrongdoing. His church denomination finally let him go, and Helena filed for divorce. Scott moved in with the other woman and eventually took a job in media, in which he excelled. Helena leaned heavily on her faith, her family, and her friends during this time and worked hard at forgiveness. She worked in continued therapy to find the underlying Soul Holes that set her up to attract and stay with a man like Scott. Why did she fall for him in the first place? Why couldn't she see the type of man he was in the beginning? Why was she so passive all those years? Then there was the trauma—the trauma of the years she spent with Scott's emotional manipulation. She would eventually fill those Soul Holes. She would learn to attract authentic love instead of its counterfeit: the User.

Users' Method of Operation

Users do not *see* you because they are too fixated on their own needs. You are not a valuable and separate individual, but a tool. They will make you feel known and understood, but that is because they study you like a salesman studies a prospect. They know your weaknesses and exploit your vulnerabilities for their purposes. Instead of being accepted and loved, you are controlled for their interest. Users do not bond or share for any reason other than to use you. Users won't mean harm, but they are careless because they are selfish. Users seek people who keep them on a pedestal. This is an unhealthy relationship that needs serious boundaries and support.

You are unseen, known, and selfishly used.

Qualities and Characteristics of a User

- Experiences great difficulty taking responsibility or blame
- Lacks sincere empathy for the hurt he's caused another
- Is defensive, blame shifting, and passionately aggressive about protecting his ego and/or reputation
- Has a strong sense of entitlement to special privileges, honors, favors, and compliance

- Has an inflated sense of self-importance and superiority
- Is largely unable to identify with others' needs if they're in conflict with his own needs
- Is exploitative in nature, willing to take advantage of other people to achieve his own goals
- Is hypersensitive to criticism or the appearance of failure
- Has a bottomless need for admiration, approval, or praise
- Discusses his own life, desires, or concerns at length while giving little or no time to listen to others
- Has a low tolerance for perceived failure, weakness, or ignorance and will lie in order to avoid being seen as such
- Expects to be given whatever he wants or feels he needs, no matter the cost to others

How it Feels to Be in a Relationship with a User

- You often wonder if you've done something to upset your partner.
- You think if you could just do a better job of meeting his needs, he would treat you better.
- You find yourself constantly trying to make him happy, especially when he's moody.
- You think constantly of him, his needs, and how to better please him.
- You feel like pleasing him is a moving target: sometimes you get it right, and other times, he becomes angry at something you've done.
- You often give up your plans or needs to meet his plans or needs.
- Sometimes you feel like you would do anything to keep him.
- You often feel afraid that he will find someone else more interesting, more beautiful, or younger than you.

- You fear that even though you give everything you have to him, he may still abandon you for someone or something else in the end.

- You don't feel whole, anchored, or secure unless you are in a relationship with a man.

- You feel anxious or guilty when you are not *with* your partner or doing something *for* your partner, as if you're doing something wrong.

- You feel like you exist to support him, and he would not make it without you.

- You feel your happiest and most powerful when you are supporting him in a successful endeavor.

- You feel awful, guilty, and anxious if you think you've disappointed him or made him angry.

- Your deflated sense of self is dependent on his inflated sense of self.

- You are preoccupied with your partner's happiness and needs.

- You find yourself excusing your partner's indiscretions, rude, or selfish behavior, even though you know they are wrong.

- Sometimes you let others take your partner's wrath so that you can remain special in his eyes.

- You find it difficult to stand up for yourself because of fear of retribution, the silent treatment, him embarrassing you in front of others, or losing freedoms.

- You don't often express a differing opinion because you will feel sliced and diced, and dumb for having that opinion.

Why You Are Attracted to Users

Over and over, I hear women in my office ask, "Why was I so naïve? How could I have been so foolish? Why didn't I stand up to him?" They wonder why they were trapped in their User's web of control. They regret the day they met their Users, the day they first said "yes," the day they first trusted. What did these women first see in their Users? What first attracted them and made them feel good enough to ignore their deepening sense of dread? What kind of spell was cast over them that made them fall head over heels in love with a man who would fool them, control them, and ultimately discard them? Their families knew. Their friends knew. Why were they blind to the User's true character?

The Importance of Your Intuition

Gavin De Becker wrote the book *The Gift of Fear* and, in it, preaches the importance of intuition. He explains that, far too often, we explain away our intuitive gut reactions designed to keep us safe from unsafe people, places, or things. Consciously, we ignore our intuition to give others the benefit of the doubt, to abstain from "judging" a book by its cover, and to believe the best about someone. This denial of our God-given instincts and overriding consciousness gets us into toxic, even dangerous, situations. De Becker writes, "What … many others want to dismiss as coincidence or a gut feeling is in fact a cognitive process, faster than we recognize and far different from the familiar step-by-step thinking we rely on so willingly. We think conscious thought is somehow better, when in fact, intuition is soaring flight compared to the plodding of logic. Nature's greatest accomplishment, the human brain, is never more efficient or invested than when its host is at risk."[12]

When at risk for engaging in a relationship with a User, you will have warning signs, bells and whistles, and yellow flashing lights. Your unconscious brain and body know that Users only use. These signals are designed to protect you. However, some of us are numb to the signs because we've been raised by Users, and we are not fully aware that we deserve better treatment. Some of us mistakenly feel obligated to give Users the benefit of the doubt, overlooking the warning signs. Still others dismiss the warning signs because a greater vacuum overrides the signal. Our Soul Holes need to be filled with adoration, affirmation, the feeling of being special to someone, and are screaming so loudly to be satisfied, we dismiss the warning signs for the promise of love. The promise the User gives us to fulfill those deep longings makes us ignore the warnings for the wishful, yet unrealistic thinking that we're being loved by a User.

The Users I've encountered have all given me ample warning signs to their true character. I have seen Users talk rudely about someone behind their back, and turn around and be sticky sweet to their face. I have heard Users ridicule someone with one breath, and speak adoringly to me in the next. I have heard Users tell one story one minute, and something totally different the next, with a rationale that makes no sense to anyone but them. Their duplicity and pretense gives you the feeling that something is off, something's not quite right, but their magnetism is unmistakable. You're not sure what it is, but you get the uneasy feeling that there's more to the

---

12 Gavin de Becker, *The Gift of Fear: and Other Survival Signals That Protect Us from Violence* (New York: Dell Publishing, 1999), 24-25.

story. There's more to the man. There's more behind the smile than meets the eye, and you're unsettled.

If you're the "forgiving" type, you might just overlook the warnings that could save you from a relationship wreck.

I, too, know the magnetizing pull of the User. The warning bells alarmed me when I met him, but I mistakenly thought, "I can handle him," until I discovered that he was the one who handled me. If you've been misled and bamboozled by a User, you're not alone. I've given the User the benefit of the doubt. I've waited too long before standing my ground. I've made excuses for the User's poor behaviors, arrogant remarks, and overly sensitive feelings. Like a thirsty girl, I got drunk on the User's charm until it made me sick. All I have to do now is smell the flattering charm of a User to remember the toxicity, and it sends me running. Once you learn and practice Living in the Pink, you'll get there too.

The User's charm is like a spider web that draws you in, but it distracts you from the more important work of exercising wisdom and prudence. The charm, the charisma, and the compliments, divert your attention away from his more disturbing characteristics.[13] Often they push for sexual activity quickly, which further clouds your discernment. Users are too good to be true, but something inside you desperately wants to believe they are that good. Somehow, the User's ability to convince you that he is special, and that you are special by proxy, is exactly what you've been dying to hear all your life. It's as if the User read the labels adorning each of your Soul Holes and devised a promise that would satisfy every single one. You know there

---

13 Dr. Jane McGregor and Tim McGregor, *The Empathy Trap: Understanding Antisocial Personalities* (London: Sheldon Press, 2013). Retrieved from http://www.sott.net/article/268449-Empathic-people-are-natural-targets-for-sociopaths-protect-yourself, 09/26/2014.

is something amiss. His duplicity bothers you, and you wonder if you can believe everything he says. The disparity between what he says and what he does is alarming, but you want to believe him, because if what he says is true, he can finally make you whole!

The User's Strategy to Get What He Wants

The User, like an actor on stage, needs props, understudies, and supporting actors. Make no mistake: there is only one lead actor, only one superstar, and that is him. The supporting actors and props are there to make him stand out, look good, meet his needs, and make him shine. How does this actor convince you to be in his play? Well, by an Oscar-winning performance, of course!

- He promises to make you his costar and let you share some of the spotlight.
- He makes you feel special—special to him and special to the world.
- He uses adoration like tear gas—he bombs you with so many compliments, you can't see what's really going on.
- He makes you feel sorry for him. He's had it hard and needs someone like you to believe in him.
- He surrounds himself with sympathetic characters—caretakers, good listeners, and sensitive types.
- He needs you, and doggone, it feels good to be needed.
- He promises you everything your desperate heart has longed for, plus some.
- He's so brimming with talent, wit, charm, and expertise, you start to believe the sky is the limit, and he's your ticket there.

Once you accept his invitation, you will start to see the dark side of this Shining Star. You started as his costar, but you quickly become a stagehand. If he ever forgets his lines, you take the blame because you didn't prepare him well enough. A star like him is under extreme pressure, so please don't ask him for any extra time. He will not tolerate being outshined, outperformed, or seen in a negative light, so you are expected to do whatever it takes to protect his impeccable image and his oh-so-fragile ego.

· ·

You started as his costar, but you quickly become a stagehand.

· ·

Taking care of his needs gives you purpose and meaning, and it is a full-time job. His enemies are your enemies, his friends are your friends, and what he says goes. His way is the best way. After all, he's the expert on these things. He has such special talent that he's convinced you to advertise it, fund it, and defend it. Your job is to *trust* him. Don't question him. Don't challenge him. Just support him, prop him up, shine the light on his good side and have ready-made excuses for his, shall we say, *imperfections.*

If you must, you can get your own stage. But be sure you are successful at what you do because you wouldn't want to bring embarrassment upon him or his reputation. If your stage is the home, then be sure to have your children pressed, prim, and proper; smart, gifted, and athletic; strong, beautiful, and anything but average! Don't go to the grocery store in your sweats. Don't leave him by himself. Keep your problems private, and never, *never* get fat!

You were invited to play a specific role, and if you do not fulfill the role adequately, remember there are other actresses who can fill the role better than you. If he doesn't remind you of this explicitly, his flirting and drifting eyes will. The Star is not held to the same standards, responsibilities, or accountabilities as the rest of the world. The Star needs special status privileges, and if you are not equipped to give him a Lifetime Special Status Pass, you should probably move on to "lesser" thespian clubs. Your needs are not important here. Don't be confused about whose needs come first.

Who Are You?

You are a compassionate person. You enjoy meeting other people's needs. You are a gifted nurturer, healer, feeler, and caretaker. You see the good in everyone. You freely give the benefit of the doubt. You trust first, ask questions later. To you, the relationship is everything. All of these wonderful qualities make you a target for the User. Lisa Scott, in her book, *It's All About Him,* would call you an Empath. "Empaths are very sensitive to suffering in the world and are often idealists who want to fix the world's problems. Empaths have an incredible capacity for self-sacrifice and are often found volunteering or dedicating time to help others. People naturally feel comfortable sharing their feelings with an Empath because of their incredible ability to feel compassion and connect with others."[14]

The shadow side of the empathic person is often an absence of a solid core. A person's *core* is a solid sense of self, the backbone, the boundary maker, the ability to recognize, legitimize, and meet one's own needs. Compassionate people can feel so strongly for and with someone else, they let themselves get swallowed up completely by the other person's needs. They rescue others from necessary difficulties. They eat the consequences of others' bad behaviors. They take on the feelings and responsibilities of others in the name of peacekeeping.

---

14 Lisa E. Scott, *It's All About Him: How to Identify and Avoid the Narcissist Male Before You Get Hurt* (Springville, UT: Cedar Fort, Inc, 2009).

Users and the Used are fiercely attracted to one another—like an unstoppable magnetic force that pulls its opposite to itself. Ross Rosenburg, a licensed counselor, describes this syndrome in his book, *The Human Magnet Syndrome*. He states that people who are codependent in nature will be, "magnetically attracted to emotional manipulators because of their opposite 'magnetic polarity.'"

- -

*Codependency is being dependent
on someone else to be okay.*

- -

Codependents have bottomless Soul Holes they want others to fill, because they feel inadequate to fill them themselves. Codependents rely on external forces for internal value. They are compelled to control people, environments, and *external* situations to bring order to their needy *internal* world. Because they don't have a solid sense of who they are, they gravitate toward someone who does. They will do almost anything to have and feel love. Their most maddening activity is taking responsibility for others' feelings of happiness, rage, depression, or fear. They mistakenly think, "If I can just make others happy, I can finally be happy myself, and all the holes in my heart will be satisfied." You can see how the User would be pleased as punch to be the recipient of all that energy!

Codependents are the perfect match for a partner who won't take responsibility for his own life. Rosenburg says, "Codependents are attracted to individuals who are either narcissistic or addicted and who neither want nor are able to fulfill their personal and emotional needs." [15] If this sounds like the User to you, you are right. Users

---

15 Ross Rosenberg, *The Human Magnet Syndrome: Why We Love People Who Hurt Us* (Eau Claire, WI: PESI Publishing and Media, 2013), 100.

like codependent people because they are so eager and willing to be used. The codependent finds her lost and underdeveloped identity wrapped up in the grandiose and inflated ego of her User—after all, the User has so much ego, there is plenty to go around!

Initially, being with a User can be a profound self-esteem boost. You may start to feel more beautiful than before, more sought after, more confident, and more intelligent. Users can make remarkable inroads to a person's self-esteem. It will feel like those empty Soul Holes start to fill. You may even say to yourself, "Wow, a guy this smart, this handsome, this confident is into *me*! It feels so good to be noticed!" But in time, your self-esteem will plummet because your efforts will never be good enough.

Christian Grey, the lecherous main character of the famed *Fifty Shades of Grey* cultural phenomenon, is a good example of a User. He is cunning, licentious, and entitled. He uses Anastasia to satisfy his deviant sexual exploits and controls her life entirely. She willingly submits to his dominance to please him. Pleasing him is her reward. Women in User relationships feel their greatest satisfaction when pleasing their Users. It's as if nothing else matters, especially themselves.

A User, like the character Christian Grey, does not see you as a separate and equal person worthy of respect and value. He sees you as an extension of himself, as someone to control, use, and exploit according to his own needs and interests. You are a prop used to sustain, feed, and enable his fragile ego. This is a hard job, because the state of his ego is as unpredictable as the weather. You most likely will feel the pressure to protect, prop up, and soothe your User partner as a pervasive and never-ending stressor. You'll feel nagging self-doubt that keeps you in a cycle of wondering, "What did I do to upset him? I should have been there, done that, said this. Is he going to get angry? Will he think I've failed him? Will he become so disappointed with me that he'll ask me to go?" You will begin to recognize no matter how supportive or submissive you are, it's never enough.

Helena's Backstory

All compassionate people come from different backgrounds with different personality types and life stories. However, let me give you an example of how one might become a perfect target for a User by telling you Helena's backstory.

Helena was raised in a Christian home; they regularly attended church. Her parents loved their children and took care of their physical and academic needs. Helena had an older sister and three younger brothers. Her sister Suzanna was like her mother: headstrong, energetic, and ambitious. Helena was like her father: passive, agreeable, and loved by everyone. They didn't have a lot of money, but, being frugal, her mother shopped at secondhand stores to buy them name-brand clothes so they wouldn't look different from their peers at school. Helena's father picked them up from school routinely with candy in his pocket for them to share. Helena enjoyed taking care of her little brothers while Suzanna played mostly with her friends.

Helena grew up in a good home, but their home was not perfect, and underlying issues set Helena up with Soul Holes she wouldn't know how to fill. Her mother regularly expressed displeasure with Helena's father for not being more assertive at work. He worked a 9-to-5 retail job for most of his life in the same town, at the same store. He never desired management or ownership; he was happy just helping the customers. Helena's mother's resentment grew, but no amount of nagging inspired him to climb the ladder. Helena's father became quiet and withdrawn at home, while her mother was angry and sharp.

As an adult, Helena recalls being badgered, threatened, and scolded by her older sister Suzanna. Was Helena her father's favorite and Suzanna her mother's? Helena thought maybe they were. Helena remembers her father hugging her too close, staring at her too long, and sometimes saying inappropriate things about her body. She wouldn't recognize these as sick sexual gestures until much later in therapy. It was hard for Helena to say one negative thing about her father or her family, even if it was true. Helena trained herself to block out the negative so efficiently, she couldn't see reality. She was in denial about how painful her childhood was.

What I gathered from listening to Helena's story was that Suzanna was nice to her when they were around their mother and father, but behind closed doors, Helena was the target of Suzanna's belittling. Helena would tell her mother and father about the treatment, but neither did enough to stop it. It was as if Suzanna was acting out her mother's anger on Helena. Suzanna was doing to Helena what her mother wished she could do to her husband. Their parents were too preoccupied with their own feelings of anger and shame to intervene on their children's behalf. Handling the dynamic occurring between their children would force them to deal with their own unresolved marital issues, which they wouldn't do. So, the bullying went on, and Helena was resigned to live her life as a victim behind closed doors.

Helena's relationship with her sister had good moments too, and Helena clung to these infrequent kindnesses. In fact, she made excuses for Suzanna, felt sorry for Suzanna, and tried to please her even more. Helena was perceptive and empathetic, and she intuitively knew that Suzanna's bitter treatment stemmed from pain. But

Suzanna's customary cruelty without parental acknowledgement or intervention resulted in Helena's extreme low self-worth. She grew up with a sense that her needs weren't important, her role was to make peace, and that bigger, better people should have all the power, while she served as the foundation beneath them.

By the time Helena was eighteen and ready to graduate high school, she was clueless about what to do with her life. She didn't know what she liked, what she wanted, or who she was. Suzanna was off at college, but Helena had no plan, no goal, and no ideas. Enter stage right: handsome Scott, freshly graduated from seminary, full of self-assurance and determination, and really into Suzanna's little sister. Scott's way of swooping Helena off her feet was rife with public displays of affection, rides on the back of his motorcycle, flowers for her mother, rounds of golf with her dad, and finally a swift, public marriage proposal on Thanksgiving Day. They would be married by Christmas.

"Wow," she thought. "He picked me! He must see something in me!" He could rescue her from having to do the hard work of healing from her past, of taking ownership of her life and desires, of finding her own feet, and standing squarely on them. By marrying into what was a familiar relationship, she wouldn't have to grow. Scott could tell her what to do and where to go and who to be. Since Scott was so confident, she wouldn't have to be. Scott could fill the holes. Scott could love her like no one else could or would, or ever wanted to. Suzanna wouldn't pick on her anymore, not with Scott there. Wouldn't Suzanna be jealous now? And Scott, and Scott, and Scott … And Scott could be God.

Why and How You Stay

After the love-bomb tear gas clears, the public adoration subsides, and the User's shiny veneer exposes the flaws underneath, you begin to see him as he really is. Even after his tireless attempts at appearing superhuman, the User is only human after all. It becomes increasingly difficult to support, prop up, and please your man. The following are **Coping Mechanisms** that partners of Users employ, hoping against hope to get their User to love them.

To get your User to love you, you …

- *Try to focus on the positive and overlook the negative.* This is the coping mechanism of **Denial** at play. You may say things to yourself like, "Well, he didn't really mean what he said," or "He had a rough day and that's why he treats me that way," or "Things really aren't that bad." You try to convince yourself that he really loves you, and that things are going to work out because 1) you're afraid that marrying him could prove to be the biggest mistake of your life, and accepting that is too painful; 2) you're afraid that displeasing him with your complaints about his behavior will only make it worse; 3) you're ultimately afraid that standing up for your needs will make him completely abandon you, leaving you more destitute than before you met him.
- *Try to work harder at meeting his needs.* You stay out of his way, predict his moods, and work till exhaustion. You stay hypervigilant to anything that could set him off and make yourself the buffer. You may have heard of the role in families with addiction, called the **Good Child**. If you can just be "the wind beneath his wings," boosting the User's ego, you think you can maintain "good-child" status with him.

- *Try to keep his true behaviors hidden from everyone else.* You **pretend** that everything is okay between you two because 1) other people just wouldn't understand that he means well; 2) if others thought poorly of him, you would feel responsible; and 3) he is so delicate, that it would crush him if others knew how it really was at home. It is your job to **protect** him.

- *Try to analyze, understand, and figure him out.* So many times, the partner of a User comes to my office because she wants to analyze her partner's behaviors. She wants to talk about her User's family of origin, his terrible mother, and his dysfunctional family. It may be fascinating, but it's completely irrelevant to actual change and growth. You want to understand your User so you can help him. But you are **over-functioning** by doing his job for him. You want him to heal more than he wants to heal. This is the codependent's way of controlling, fixing, and counseling her partner. But it backfires and makes the User feel demeaned and resentful, resulting in angry outbursts, put downs, and public ridicule.

- *Provoke him so you can feel love.* Once you tire of trying and failing to please him, you provoke him just to feel love. You **act out**. You "forget" to run that errand. You are short with him at the dinner table. You make a jab at him in public. You flirt with his best friend. You certainly know how to get a rise out of him, and the argument that ensues is fueled by anger and disappointment over broken promises. It is *intensity* that results, but it was *intimacy* you were wanting. Chances are it is you who ends up apologizing "for making him mad," without any real relationship resolution.

- *Try to convince him of your importance.* You exhaustingly try to explain yourself, your decisions, and your feelings because if you can just get him to understand your needs, then maybe your needs will be valid. You are an **approval junkie**, and you need *external* approval before you give yourself *internal* approval. You don't believe you can validate yourself. You believe that he must recognize, bless, and give permission for your needs to be met. You try to convince your User of something you don't completely believe yourself—that you are worthy of love.

- *Cling to the good in him.* And really there is some. You've seen his kindness, his generosity, his patience. Maybe it's for other people, and not for you, but you still see it. Users are not *bad* people. Users are *just* people. The trouble is that the Users don't truly believe they are *just* people like the rest of messed-up humanity; they believe they are special and better. You've had to buy into the **Big Lie** that he is above reproach, untouchable, and unaccountable. But the truth is, Users lack the basic character traits that make healthy relationships possible, such as humility, ability to admit wrong, forthright honesty, and, above all, empathy. Without these traits, no matter how much good you see in your User, he will be utterly incapable of a healthy relationship with you unless and until he develops these traits.

Because you have so many coping mechanisms to help you survive, you may resign yourself to staying with your User indefinitely. You'd like to do more than just survive, but you feel hopeless about true change. You recognize that you will be doing all the emotional work of the relationship. You will be doing the heavy lifting of child raising. You will be "covering a multitude of sins."

You do it maybe because you don't believe you're worth more, or because it's your "God-given duty," or because he would die without you, and you'd feel so guilty about breaking his heart. You do it so he won't leave you. But what do Users do? They use you until you're used up, and then they move on to use someone else. Slowly, you die inside. You see that what you thought was "surviving" is your own slow death.

It doesn't have to be this way. You don't have to just survive. You can *thrive*. You can break the codependent patterns of trying to please, protect, financially provide for, and prop up your partner. You can learn new ways of interacting with your partner that instill self-respect, true intimacy, and unconditional love. The following is a diagram that explains the inner motivations of Users and the People-Pleasing Partners they marry. You'll see that fear drives the User/People Pleasing relationship, ultimately resulting in feelings of abandonment.

User and People Pleasing Paradigm[16]

User Paradigm	People-Pleasing Paradigm	Healthy Paradigm
Fear—of being seen as unworthy and suffering abandonment.	**Fear**—I don't want to hurt or upset his fragile ego for fear of his ultimate anger or hatred toward me.	**Love**—Love casts out all fear. Because I am loved, I am not motivated by fear.
Idolatry—I deserve worship because I am better than you.	**Idolatry**—I live to make him feel special.	**Appropriate Worship**—No human is worthy of my worship above my devotion to God.
Shame—I must be the best, smartest, most successful, or I am nothing.	**Shame**—I struggle with low self-esteem and feelings of unworthiness.	**Self-Acceptance**—Because I accept myself as-is, I can accept others too.
Competition—I measure my value as compared to other people.	**Competition**—I never seem to measure up compared to others.	
Control—I must manipulate people and things to avoid my shame.	**Control**—I control others through guilt, and keep the peace by making excuses for him.	**Collaboration**—Instead of seeing myself one-up or one-down from others, I am able to work with them as equals.
Denial—I use blame and criticism to avoid the truth of my selfish actions.	**Denial**—It's not really that bad. I can handle it.	**Self-Control**—I control myself, not others.
Abandonment—No matter the idolatrous devotion of others, I will still feel abandoned and alone.	**Abandonment**—I abandoned my own needs and attach myself to an abandoning person.	**Belonging**—Because I refuse to abandon myself, I find intimacy with God.

---

16 Idolatry used here means to worship someone or something other than God. When we honor God above others, then we agree with God's natural order of things. We see people as equals, not greater or less than ourselves. We have reasonable expectations of others and ourselves, and see God as a Source of life instead of others.

Steps to Living in the Pink

When I was fourteen years old, I spent the summer with a friend named Debbie. Debbie's house was perched on a hill, five miles away from mine. Almost every day, I biked that hill to get to her house. We hung out at the pool, watched *Days of Our Lives*, ate mac 'n' cheese, and memorized every word on Dcf Lcppard's *Hysteria* album. I thought we were best friends. But when I saw her on the first day of ninth grade, she pretended not to notice me. When I tried to sit with her at lunch, she said she was saving that seat for someone else. I discovered that Debbie's *real* best friend was back from California, and I was no longer needed to help Debbie pass the long and lonely summer days. This was my first lesson with a User, but not my last.

Since then, I've learned the healthy habits of forever friends, lifetime lovers, and the happily married. I know now what I didn't know then: improving a relationship, even a relationship with a User, starts with me. I wonder what would have happened if I told Debbie early in the summer of 1987, "I've ridden my bike to your house three times in a row, and I want you to come to my house this time." What if she had? The bike ride to my house would have been easy-peazy, but going back up the five-mile hill would have changed her perspective. Would she have respected me more given the sacrifices I was making for our friendship? If I had given her a chance to respect me early on, would she have respected me on the first day of ninth grade? I'll never know, because I never once asked her to make that ride.

As insignificant as this junior high interaction may seem, it illustrates the simplicity of the principle. True and authentic relationship is a mutual exchange of energy, sacrifice, and love. If it's one-sided, it's not true. I know now that I have the power to change the dynamic, to change the atmosphere, to change the relationship results. The same is true for you. Change starts with you. You'll never know just how much power you have to change your relationship unless you take the first step.

Step 1: Assess which of your Vital Three Needs are not being met. More than likely, if you are with a User, your need to be *seen* as a separate and valuable person has been neglected.

But it hasn't been neglected by your partner alone. It's been neglected by *you*.

If you *saw* yourself as valuable, unique, and worthy of respect, you wouldn't have attracted a User or kept him around for so long. Sometimes we do to ourselves what's always been done to us. If we were overlooked or under-prioritized in our family of origin, we learn ways of treating ourselves the same way.

You have the power to change! You have the power to fill that original Soul Hole.

Here are some questions to bring awareness to that original unmet need:

- What needs did I have as a child that went unmet? (emotional, scholastic, social, physical, spiritual, etc.)
- What prevented my parents from meeting those needs? (addiction, depression, warped priorities, mental illness, poverty, poor choices, etc.)
- What would have made me feel *seen* back then? (to feel like a priority, to be able to share needs and have them matter, to feel okay even if I messed up or failed, etc.)
- What did I need to hear from my parents back then? (you are loved; you are wanted; you are fun, pretty, and lovable; you are worth it; you are worthy of love; you are not a nuisance; you are not a problem; you are not a disappointment; you are special to me; you are seen, etc.)

- What needs do I have right now that I can see and meet but am choosing not to? (health, friendship, support groups, counseling, financial advice, legal advocacy, education, pastoral prayer and support, etc.)
- What ways can I value myself today? (form and verbalize my own opinions and decisions, speak up for what I need and want, recognize when I'm doing too much for others and step back, schedule "me" time, stop ignoring myself, talk kindly to myself, etc.)

Step 2: List Specific Actions to Boost Your Self-Respect. It's one thing to read about taking care of yourself; it's another thing entirely to do it.

. . . .

You cannot __will__ yourself into love. You must __behave__ yourself into it.

. . . .

You cannot just tell yourself you're worthy of love enough times until you finally believe it; you must *act* that way and trust the feelings will follow. Here are some REPS you can start practicing today.

R Restore order through boundaries

You will need to say no to several things that drain your energy, your value, and your time. Consider the following passage from Proverbs:

"My son, pay attention to what I say; listen closely to my words. Do not let them out of your sight, keep them within your heart; for they are life to those who find them and health to a man's whole body. *Above all else, guard your heart, for it is the wellspring of life.* Put away perversity from your mouth; keep corrupt talk far from your lips. Let your eyes look straight ahead; fix your gaze directly before you. Make level paths for your feet and take only ways that are firm. Do not swerve to the right or the left; keep your foot from evil."[17] (emphasis mine)

This advice demands confidence, and so does setting boundaries. Saying "no" can be very scary because of the feared consequences. However, if confidently setting firm boundaries, as this passage instructs, results in the wellspring of life and health to the body, then you have nothing to fear.

1. Boundaries with Self Care

Prioritize good self-care. Recognize when you are overwhelmed, burned out, and in need of help or rest. Make a plan to take care of your health, your diet, your body, your interests, and your heart. By taking care of yourself, you allow others to do the necessary work to take care of themselves too, instead of you doing it for them. Ignoring healthy boundaries and healthy self-respect is abandoning yourself. Don't do to *yourself* what others have done to you.

2. Boundaries with Communication

It is also important to set communication boundaries with your partner. He is most likely using tactics to snare you into pointless arguments, and requiring you to take the blame that is not yours. He may even be using bullying tactics to get his way, to avoid facing his own issues, or to look or feel superior. You will need to communicate to your partner that the old way of doing things is not going to happen anymore.

Conversation with Expectations and Consequences

Say, "*I realize that we haven't communicated well over the years. Some of that is my fault and I'm working on that. However, some of it is your fault,*

---

17 Prv 4:20-27 (New International Version).

and I need you to work on it too. I need to be treated with respect from this point on. I will no longer tolerate _____ (list the behaviors here, such as name calling, raging, belittling, yelling, blame shifting, sarcasm, badgering, judging, criticizing, threatening, etc.) If you continue to do these things, I will _____ _____ (list the consequences you deem appropriate, like walk away from the conversation, leave the house to restore my sense of peace, expect you to move into the guest bedroom, expect you to move out, expect you to apologize to the kids for how you spoke to me, will meet with the pastor and speak to him about what's going on, will require you to seek individual counseling, will talk to a lawyer about separation and/ or divorce, etc.)"

Broken Record

Stating these boundaries and consequences out loud requires a lot of strength. Congratulate yourself for taking an important step. After a deserved pat on the back, buckle in for his resistance. You will need to enact **follow through** with consequences, resist the temptation to engage in unhealthy conversations, and ignore his attempts to hook you into fruitless fights. You may need to repeat your expectations and consequences over and over like a broken record to avoid arguments or to remain unhooked.

E Experience God through deeper dependence

Some of us are so exhausted by our busy, chaotic lives, that we are too tired or guilt-ridden to connect with God. Some of us feel undeserving of His help, or just plain confused about what we believe. Others are angry with God for the pain and trauma they've experienced. These are normal responses. I have one principle that *always* works for every person in every situation:

Just Show Up. Be real. Be honest. Be human. And show up. The spiritual life is about experiencing God, feeling His love, and loving Him back. But often we substitute the *relationship* with God with the *duties* of life. We forget that our soul needs as much attention as our to-do list.

Trauma has a way of cutting us off from ourselves, and as a result, we can feel far from God too. Relationship trauma can cause so much internal pain, we isolate ourselves and feel utterly alone in the world. You may have experienced a series of traumas in your relationships, and the pain feels too deep to start uncovering. Opening yourself up to the Loving Presence of God is the first step in healing and trusting yourself again.

"Come to me, all you who are weary and burdened, and I will give you rest. Take my yoke upon you and learn from me, for I am gentle and humble in heart, and you will find rest for your souls. For my yoke is easy and my burden is light."[18]

Here are a couple ways to experience God by just showing up:

1. Journal: Journaling slows your thoughts down to the speed you can write. This is helpful when you feel emotionally flooded or triggered. Journal your thoughts, feelings, and disappointments, and address them to God. Journaling helps you see your thoughts and feelings as valuable, to know yourself intimately, and to share yourself with the God Who accepts you unconditionally. Anything goes here. Try not to filter yourself. Just write from the heart and see what comes up.

Journaling is especially helpful when you are angry or stressed and can't focus on anything else but what's troubling you. Once you

---

18 Matthew 11:28-30 NIV

get it on paper, you can leave it there and attend to other things, like being present for your kids, yourself, and your work.

Journaling is also a way to nurture yourself. By taking the time to put your thoughts, feelings, and fears on paper, you are communicating to yourself, "My heart is important. I want to listen to it and give it freedom to feel. I want to validate what's going on in there."

2. Dependence Prayers: Is it cheesy to pray the Carrie Underwood song, "Jesus, Take the Wheel?" Well, call me Queen of Cheese, because I come back to this prayer a lot. When women think about asking God for help, they have a running checklist of shortcomings that stand in their way. Guilt accuses them saying, "You only come to God when you need something. Why should God listen to you now?" or "You deserve the problems you're having. You're the one who made all the bad decisions." They feel as though they don't deserve to come to God with their problems.

I find this passage helpful: "Let us then approach the throne of grace with confidence, so that we may receive mercy and find grace to help us in our time of need."[19] You may be used to white-knuckling through difficulties because asking for help was seen as weak, or just not permitted. Asking God for help may be a new possibility for you, and it may take a little practice to cultivate.

When you are confused, upset, or stressed, simply ask God to help you. By doing this, you are admitting you don't have it all together, and that you need God's help. This is the simplest (and fastest!) form of humility. Depending on God, moment by moment for everything we need, makes us aware of how our limitations are met with His provision. Dependence Prayers invite God to prove

---

19 Heb 4:16 (New International Version).

that we are seen, known, and unconditionally accepted just by the simple act of leaning on Him.

The bible says, "He guides the humble in what is right and teaches them His way."[20]

Just because you didn't spend an hour in prayer this morning, doesn't disqualify you from saying quick prayers throughout your day. Just because you haven't been to church for years, or you don't even know what you believe, doesn't mean you can't pray to God for help. God gets that we are human, that we make mistakes, and that we need Him day by day, moment by moment.

You must come to view your dependence on God as the only thing keeping you sane and functioning. By experiencing God through deeper dependence, you will begin to thrive. Instead of looking for your User to be pleased with you, look to God. Your User is dethroned from the highest place in your heart, and God replaces him.

Good questions to ask yourself are:

1. Who am I really living for?
2. Who is my source of provision and love?
3. What blocks my relationship with God?
4. How can I stop getting in the way of God's plan?
5. Why do I need to be the rescuer, healer, savior, or helper to feel okay?
6. What peace and freedom does God have for me if I give up control?
7. How does God want me to feel about myself? (Hint: really good! God wants you to be at peace with yourself and others,

---

20 Ps 25:9 (New International Versions).

but you can't be if you spend your time trying to fix them, prop them up, control them, or save them.)

P Provide yourself with people

You may have been tempted to keep your User's bad behavior a secret, but you'll find that sharing the truth with trusted people is empowering. The people in your life will probably suspect that your User is not everything he'd like everyone to believe. Don't let shame, embarrassment, or obligation to protect his reputation keep you from getting the support you need.

You will need a lot of emotional support and connection with safe sisters. Because you can't *be there* for yourself 100% of the time, you need others to be there for you. When you are just beginning to set appropriate boundaries and say "no" more often, you will need lots of encouragement from others. Check into programs like Celebrate Recovery,[21] Codependents Anonymous,[22] and individual counseling to help you kick the habit of being codependent with your User. Investing time and money into these worthy exercises solidifies your value. When you put time and money into something that is *just* for you, you slowly begin to believe you are worth every minute and penny. Tell your support system what you are working on, and give them specific ways they can support you.

S Seek intimacy in the context of counseling

This may seem counterintuitive when you're trying to set boundaries with your User. Actually, seeking intimacy is a necessary step in personal growth as much as relational growth, if it's done in the context

---

21 www.celebraterecovery.com
22 www.coda.org

of counseling. You cannot know if your partner wants to change alongside you unless you seek true intimacy with him. Remember, true intimacy is:

- Knowing and expressing your feelings in non-accusatory language
- Sharing weaknesses, fears, and vulnerabilities without fear of judgment or control
- Validating your partner's experiences and feelings without judging, controlling, changing, or taking them personally

How can you share with your partner, especially if your User is self-absorbed, self-righteous, and used to you being subservient? You tell him what you want in the safety of good counseling. Your counselor should be able to recognize his attempts at manipulating your emotions to get his own way and will keep you emotionally safe in the process.

One of your main goals from counseling is to be heard and validated by your partner. If he learns to be empathetic with your needs and feelings, then he may also learn the skills of accountability.

Accountability

Users are not motivated by empathy, guilt, or morality. They are motivated by consequences to their ego. Your efforts at explaining your feelings or your needs do little to impact his behavior, yet explaining is where most women stop. It is important to hold your partner accountable with the above suggested consequences. For your User to become an involved and loving partner, he must be able to:

1. Be accountable for his actions without making excuses or justifications
2. Be eager to apologize with humility and true repentance

3. Refuse to blame others for his own shortcomings
4. Treat you and your stated boundaries with respect
5. Be a willing participant in learning empathy skills.

Tell Him What You Expect in Counseling

It is good for you to identify your needs and wants, and it is especially good for you to verbalize them. When this is done in a heathy counseling environment, you will be able to hold yourself intact while expressing what you need to say.

This step is less important for him to hear, and more important for you to say. This step is for *you.* This step builds your self-respect and strengthens your resolve. Here is an example of how it can be done:

Say, "I know we haven't been seeing eye to eye, and some of it is my fault (humility and ownership of your stuff). I've been defensive, and angry, and even unloving at times (identifying your stuff). I'm working on those things and want to change them through counseling and Celebrate Recovery (list measurable goodwill action items). I feel like I'm missing the real you, the you deep down inside (effort toward intimacy). I miss the closeness, the teamwork, and the good times. I miss *you* (vulnerability). I'm with you because I genuinely love you. I want us to learn how to be partners. I want us to learn how to be close in a healthy way instead of the way we've been doing it. Would you be willing to _____ (now name the measurable action items that you want him to do, i.e., individual counseling, AA, Substance Abuse treatment, porn-addiction treatment, marriage counseling, etc.)?

This is a simple example of seeking intimacy without losing yourself. You may need to practice these kinds of conversations in many different scenarios until you are proficient. You can practice with the piano teacher who is consistently late, the cashier that overcharged you, or your daughter who hasn't been doing her chores.

WARNING: *Your User will likely not join you in your attempts at healthy intimacy.* He may say something like, "You're always telling me what to do. You're never satisfied—you always want more. There's no way I'm doing counseling or one of those programs! I'm not going to waste my time when I'm not the one with the problem, you are!" A good couples counselor will know immediately what he is trying to do and will intervene so you are heard.

Or he may say, "Sure," but never follow through. Your counselor is a third party to hold him accountable.

If your User gets defensive, angry, evades responsibility, blames you, brings up other things to argue about, uses sarcasm, changes the topic, or never follows through, he is giving you your answer. His answer is "no" to healthy intimacy. If he is unwilling to honor your expectations or to self-correct through consequences, then his answer is "No."

I'm sorry to say that Users must be willing to go through lengthy overhauls, rock-bottom, come-to-Jesus experiences before they are willing, let alone able, to join in healthy intimacy. Many will make the choice to stay just as they are, instead of doing the necessary work to have healthy relationships.

When you can say the statements above anger-free, and with plenty of confidence, you will have completed your task. You will have owned your stuff, worked on changing your stuff, and invited him to join you on the healthy road to intimacy. He very well could turn you down, spit on your offer, or just find someone else to prop him up since you're no longer willing. His rejecting response doesn't mean that your offer of healthy intimacy wasn't good enough, you didn't say it right, or that you are not worth his effort. It just means that *he is unable and/or unwilling to receive the offer.* He has been hiding from intimacy behind a veil of control and ego for so long, he can't recognize a good deal when he sees one. But you will rest easy at the end of the day, knowing you gave him the opportunity.

While You're Waiting for Him to Make up His Mind... Learn to:

- **Self-soothe in healthy ways** such as enjoying your own hobbies, creating something, playing a sport, listening to your favorite music, talking with friends, and having things to look forward to.
- **Follow through with consequences to broken boundaries.** Setting boundaries is one thing; following through with them is another. Make sure you stay strong with these limits and consequences.
- **Invest in Codependency Recovery.** Your User has gotten away with bad behavior and poor treatment of you for a long time. You've adapted codependent coping patterns to deal with this poor treatment, and unlearning codependency is essential.
- **Schedule positivity to neutralize the negative.** Read, watch, and listen to positive material with good messages so you can stay positive. So much of your relationship can drain you; limit the other things in your life from doing the same.
- **Forgive yourself for the relationship mistakes you've made.** Shame can kill a woman's confidence, so don't let it overwhelm you during this critical period. Shame sounds like, "I shouldn't have ever married him; why was I so blind? I've been such a fool. What if he's right? What if no man could ever love me? It's too late for me. I'm nothing. I'm

too scarred. It's over for me." These are shame triggers that could derail your progress. Make sure you correct the shame messages with, "I may have made mistakes, but I'm making good choices now. I made the best decisions I could with the information I had. I can't do anything about the past, but I can do my best today. I can take good care of myself."

And What if He Changes... But Only a Little?

Some women find themselves at an impasse at this point. Her partner is willing to change a little, or do the bare minimum, but not anything more than what he must to stay married. She must decide how much she can tolerate, and for how long. She must decide if his attempts are so menial, that she actually feels worse about herself settling. She may feel that he is just playing more games to control her. These women often must feel that God *releases* them from their User marriage before they are free to divorce.

Many women ask God what He wants them to do. I believe that God often returns the question back to them, "What do *you* want?"

· ·

This is often the last question you'll want to answer. It's the one you've been avoiding all your life.

· ·

It was never safe or encouraged for you to *want* anything, or to *need* anything. You lived according to other people's wants and needs. God offers you the choice to finally answer this for yourself. It is very healing for you to have this opportunity to voice your decision. Unlike others in your past, God honors your wants and needs, even if you're not 100% sure of them. I often hear women answer this question with tears, saying, "I want to be free," or "I want this to end," or "I want to be released from this treatment." Your needs and wants matter.

What if They Refuse to Be Accountable for Their Role?

Sometimes divorce should be considered a gift from God—a way out of a contract when the contract has been broken by the other party. Divorce can be a gift to the person in the relationship who is continually being used up for the other person's gain. The marriage contract has been broken spiritually, emotionally, and physically long before the papers are signed. A relationship where one person uses the other, is not a marriage. It's exploitation. It is a one-sided vampiric relationship with consumption as its primary objective. Divorce can be a gift to the person who is on the verge of being all used up, exhausted from being the only adult in the relationship, and tired of holding everything together. That kind of relationship is not a marriage. It's a one-up one-down, parasitic-host relationship that results in you losing yourself.

Users cannot engage in true intimacy until they learn to see you as a separate and equal individual worthy of love and respect. You are responsible for taking the first step toward your own self-love and self-respect. You can do it! You are worth it!

Step 3: Space, Time, and Separation

Once you see your own self-worth, you may quickly lose patience for your User's vampiric treatment. It's as if the fog clears, the numbing agent wears off, and you come to your senses. The light of the truth, that you are worthy of respect and love, shines so brightly on you; you will become disgusted at the foul state of affairs around you. You may be astonished at just how little you really meant to him. You may be shocked at yourself for tolerating his mistreatment for so long.

One thing is certain: you realize that this toxic pattern must stop. Often your User's manipulative tendencies are difficult, if not impossible, to change. Your partner must see that the way he engages in relationship is as unhealthy and destructive, and has no use in the real world. If your User is unwilling to own his stuff and make significant actions toward healing and recovery, you must create distance between you so you are no longer the target of his exploitation.

You cannot change him or control him. And you certainly cannot "help" him as long as you are a part of the unhealthy system. Remove yourself from it, and let God do the work of convicting him.

Space, time, and separation look different in every situation. Some women will move into another bedroom or ask their partner to do so. Some women move in with a trusted family member for a while or get their own apartment. Some decide that they need more advanced and permanent separation, like divorce, to feel emotionally, financially, and sexually secure again.

While pursuing emotional distance, avoid giving him books to read, asking him to go to church with you, sending him a sermon or a scripture that you think will "encourage" him, giving him opportunities to connect with you, hinting about his drinking problem, or checking up if he is going to small group meetings. You are over-functioning. Stop. Your energy should not go to the relationship at this point; it should go to your own self-care and healing.

While you're pursuing physical distance, avoid contact. Really, just avoid contact. Simple, right? Probably not. Your User will think of countless "necessary" reasons to see you. Avoid these as much as possible, or insist the meetings be in public at a neutral setting or with a third party. You are not a bad person for not wanting to see him or have contact with him. The more contact you have with him, the more temptation you will feel to reengage in your old, unhealthy patterns. You will need emotional distance to recognize and stop unhealthy patterns.

Your User may have the capacity to truly love, and with therapy, patience, and long-term practice, you may see your User show signs of true change. He may learn to recognize his manipulation, his self-centered behaviors, and the detrimental pull of an overindulged ego. He may truly start to heal the insecurity that drives him. If he does, you will see evidence of this change of heart. You will see him being humble instead of angry, mature instead of manipulative, and accountable instead of blaming. Full trust can only be reestablished with consistent evidence of change over time.

Not many Users are willing to make those changes. Most choose ego over relationship. He will either hit rock bottom with his addiction, failures, finances, or family, or he'll find someone else to use.

Remember Christian Grey from *Fifty Shades of Grey*? The trilogy ends with Anastasia happily raising a family with her User, Christian. The series seemed to resolve with Anastasia's love as Christian's cure for deviance and abusive control. However, Anastasia was *still afraid* of Christian throughout their relationship—afraid to displease him, disobey him, or make him angry. There is no happy ending for a woman who is afraid of her partner. Happy endings with a User only happen in fictional stories. The reality is much more painful.

The next group will and should scare you right out of your comfortable Danskos. They are not to be toyed with, entertained willingly, or treated in any way except with extreme caution. They are the Abusers.

Chapter 6

ABUSERS: This Ain't Love, Baby

Farewell, ungrateful traitor,
Farewell, my perjured swain,
Lent never injured creature
Believe a man again.
The pleasure of possessing
Surpasses all expressing,
But 'tis too short a blessing,
And love too long a pain.

—John Dryden[23]

Don't envy violent people
   or copy their ways.
Such wicked people are detestable to the LORD,
   but he offers his friendship to the godly.[24]

Behind the closed doors of American households, in suburban neighborhoods and inner-city slums, in backwater hills, and

---

23 John Dryden, "Farewell, Ungrateful Traitor," Emile Capouya, *Classic English Love Poems* (New York: Hippocrene Books, 1998), p.61.
24 Pr 3:31-32 (New Living Translation).

down the street from your house, in elevators and in penthouse suites, a woman is afraid for her life. Her partner, though loving sometimes, is someone different when no one else is looking. He hits her, pushes her, and sometimes kicks her too. The brutal force he wields could level another man his size, but another man is not the target. It's her. The threat of violence haunts her like a ghost, trailing her through the grocery store, the commute to work, the carpool at school, around the family dinner table. Its darkness is never far away. Its inevitability mocks her every move. The random and unpredictable violence from the hands of the man she loves is always threatening, always lingering in a cross word, a bad day, a misunderstood text, an unwanted email from an old boyfriend, a nosy neighbor, or one drink too many. The rage is just a breath away. She wonders if someday that breath will be her last.

The reality is that one in four women will experience domestic violence at some point in their lifetime. This may be difficult to fathom if you've experienced a violence-free home. Not everyone has. Some homes breed a culture of violence until it becomes the norm. Violence begets violence. Without help, girls who witness domestic violence are more vulnerable to abuse as teens and adults. Without intervention, boys who witness domestic violence are far more likely to become adult abusers to their partners and children.[25]

Every year, of the women who are victims of homicide, one in three is murdered by her current or former partner. What was supposed to be love turns out to be rage. What was supposed to be comfort, turns out to be control, sometimes with deadly consequences. The person you are supposed to trust is the least trustworthy of all.

---

25 Finkelhor, David; Turner, Ormrod, Hamby and Kracke et al., National Survey of Children's Exposure to Violence, OJJDP, *Juvenile Justice Bulletin* (October 2009).

Psychological abuse, such as threatening rage, name-calling, emotional manipulation, and hostile intimidation is just as damaging as physical abuse and occurs more than we know. One in four college women report surviving rape (twenty-five percent) or attempted rape (twelve percent) since their fourteenth birthday.[26] In a study by the U.S. Centers for Disease Control, of 5,000 college students at over 100 colleges, 20 percent of women answered "yes" to the question, "In your lifetime, have you been forced to submit to sexual intercourse against your will?"[27] Often, the abuse goes unreported because of the shame associated with being abused by someone you love. Sometimes, the victims of abuse and rape consider suicide because of the shame and pain the abuse has caused.[28]

The MO of the Abuser

The Abuser *sees* you and *knows* you but his affection is *false.*

The difference between Users and Abusers is malice.

You are *seen* and valued so you can be controlled.

You are *known* to gain your allegiance.

What feels like love in the beginning, you realize is malice in the end. The Abuser deals in confusion and keeps you feeling scared, hated, and small, and alternately cherished, special, and needed. The Abuser manipulates your feelings to be whatever he needs them to be in the moment to achieve his goals. Abusers are malicious and often will stop at nothing to stay in control of you.

You are Seen, Known, and Maliciously Controlled.

---

26 Robin Warshaw, *I Never Called it Rape* (New York: HarperCollins Publishers, 1994).
27 K. A. Douglas et al. "Results From the 1995 National College Health Risk Behavior Survey," *Journal of American College Health* 46 (1997): 55-66.
28 Warshaw, *I Never Called it Rape.*

April's Backstory

Remember April from the opening story of the book? April was an independent, single young woman who loved God, her friends, and her family. She was active in her church and in volunteering. She graduated college and had good contract work. All these things were signs of her personal happiness and success. How could she ever end up with a guy like Seth, on the brink of financial collapse and homelessness? What made her susceptible to his manipulation? What made her look past his glaring character flaw toward violence?

April's Soul Holes are like many of yours. They started when she was young, empty, and yearning for true fulfillment. As a child, her father took little interest in her, giving most of his limited attention to her older brothers. Young girls were a mother's work. He wasn't very good at bonding, playing, or showing affection with children. She didn't get to experience the healthy attachment necessary for emotional well-being, like pony rides on her daddy's knee, bedtime cuddles, or playful tea parties. In fact, if you ask her about any early memories of her father, she would report not having any at all. She remembers admiring her daddy and wanting him to notice her, but never quite figuring out what would make him turn her way.

Once she hit puberty, her father started to take notice of her, especially if her presence or appearance reflected negatively on him at church. He disapproved of her choice of clothing, said she was trying to look too sexy, and frequently made her change minutes before leaving for church. He disapproved of her friends and actively sabotaged her friendships. He "forgot" to give her their phone messages. He was rude to the friends who called. He disapproved of her attitude and shouted hateful names across the dinner table. They argued incessantly. All the attention she needed as a young girl was steamrolled over her, now that she was a budding young woman, with criticism and accusations.

In a vacuum of need, the negativity spawned extreme self-doubt. She knew his controlling attitude didn't feel like love, but it was all she knew. The attention she was getting from boys now was usually sexual in nature. It surprised her that boys found her attractive and interesting. The attention felt great.

Leroy, a twenty-two-year-old man, helped with the youth group and lived nearby. His father and April's father served on the church board together. Leroy drove April to and from youth group, oftentimes alone in his car. When she was fourteen years old, she noticed her body responding to his hugs at youth group. She was thrilled when he sat next to her at events, when they shared the piano bench when practicing worship songs, and when he volunteered to drive her home in his car. She loved the attention she was getting from him, and why not? She'd been aching for attention from a man her entire life. One night, before driving her home after a church function, he sexually assaulted her.

Bewildered and naïve, she asked, "What are you doing?"

He answered, "We are having sex with our clothes on, or at least some of them."

She had never kissed a boy, and now she was shocked by how far he was going. She didn't want to lose his special attention, but she didn't like what he was doing to her either. She had such mixed feelings of desire and shame and wanting to be wanted. She desperately wanted to please him—but she knew this didn't seem right. Once he dropped her off at her house that night, she didn't feel special anymore. She just felt dirty and used.

April's father found a love letter in the mail box a few days later from April to Leroy. In the living room that night, he opened it and read it aloud for her mother and her to hear. April hung her head in humiliation and lied that nothing ever happened between them. She just had a silly crush on him, and she didn't know why she wrote it; she must be stupid. At all cost, she would never betray Leroy or tell anyone what he had done. She was grounded from youth group. She was forbidden to talk to the young man again.

"You should feel ashamed of yourself writing a letter to a twenty-two-year-old like that."

It never occurred to April that she was not the one to blame. It never occurred to her that her parents never should have allowed a twenty-two-year-old man, still living with his parents, to drive their fourteen-year-old daughter home from church every week. It never occurred to her that her youth pastor never should have allowed a twenty-two-year-old man to cozy up to a fourteen-year-old girl week after week, practice worship songs at the piano together, or stay up late talking after events. It never occurred to April that her parents sought to maintain an untarnished reputation among the church leadership, and April was scapegoated to carry the shame so church leadership could save face. All April knew was that if her parents really knew about what happened that night in the car, they would confirm what she already felt—that she was a slut and a whore and a Jezebel. And maybe they did know but turned a blind eye so that awkward confrontations would not have to be made.

April's first sexual experience was with an Abuser. In the absence of her father's affection, she came alive to Leroy, and later to Seth. She learned to hold secrets and to protect her abusers. She learned to make excuses for them and to see them in a different light than other people saw them. After all, what she got from them was the closest thing to love she had ever experienced from a man. From her experience with Leroy, she paired "feeling wanted" with "being used." From her parents, she learned she was not worth protecting, not worth fighting for, or paying attention to. The value she brought to the family was to make them look good at church and to bear the burden of guilt inside if she did anything less.

When Seth came along, she was already primed to be groomed, courted, love-bombed, schmoozed, and sold a bill of goods. She was completely unable to see Seth for the Abuser he was, because no one ever told her that what she experienced with Leroy was abuse. She was not aware that what she experienced from her parents and her church was verbal abuse and emotional neglect. What she experienced with people like Leroy and Seth was not true love at all. It was sick and twisted abuse for their own pleasure. Yes, April. You did love them. You loved them well. But they never loved you back.

Macy's Story

Macy was a fifteen-year-old freshman in high school when her world turned upside down. Macy's parents were fighting a lot at home, and didn't have any extra energy to tend to Macy's life and needs. She'd come home after school with common freshman feelings of inadequacy, anxiety, and loneliness but didn't have a healthy outlet to share those feelings. She was overwhelmed with the amount of schoolwork she had.

To make everything worse, her best friend moved to a new school, leaving Macy feeling vulnerable and alone. She started hanging out with a new group of kids—the kind that skipped class, smoked weed, and had little parental oversight. She told herself she wouldn't let her grades slip and she wouldn't become a druggie, but it felt good to be accepted as a part of the group. Macy's mom was drinking a lot at night, which made Macy feel lonely, so she started going over to other kids' houses to get away. That's where she met Alex, her friend's nineteen-year-old brother. Alex seemed to like Macy right away. Macy felt special that an older guy thought she was pretty enough to talk to.

Over the course of a year, her infatuation with Alex grew. He texted her from time to time and sometimes would call her and talk for up to an hour. He would empathize about what jerks her parents were, and how beautiful she was, and how lucky the boys in her class were. No guy her own age said these things. Guys her own age barely even noticed her. Alex moved out of his parent's house which gave him more freedom to see Macy when and wherever he wanted. Macy wouldn't hear from him for weeks, and then he would text her and ask if he could pick her up. Why not? Her mom and dad probably wouldn't notice she was gone.

Alex talked Macy into doing things that she had never considered before—posing barely clothed, taking pictures, and drinking vodka to feel more comfortable. She felt conflicted. She knew it wasn't right, but her feelings for him were so strong, she couldn't say "no." She tried to say "no" once, and he pushed her onto the bed, threw her clothes at her, and told her to catch a bus home. She hated making him mad. She wouldn't say "no" again. She hated the feeling of being rejected by him.

Alex had parties at his new place, where drugs and alcohol were widely available. On Macy's sixteenth birthday, Alex fixed her a cocktail of ecstasy and alcohol to get her high. Alex collected money from two of his friends at the party and let them take Macy into a locked room. It became a birthday she would never want to remember.

This happened again and again, and when Macy tried to refuse, Alex would take her by the hair and slam her head into the wall. He threatened to send videos of her to her friends at school. He threatened to hurt her little brother. He told her she was dirt and that she was lucky he paid any attention to her at all. She wondered how it got so bad, and how it got so far.

Finally, Macy's grades, depression, and drug use caught the attention of her parents. Once the truth of Alex's abusive and illegal treatment sobered them into taking action, they went to the police to press charges against Alex. It turns out Alex wasn't nineteen when he met Macy; he was twenty-four. Further investigation found he was doing the same thing to two other girls just like Macy. He lured impressionable girls with family problems by promising love and attention. He groomed vulnerable girls to do whatever he wanted them to do by making them feel special, sexy, loved, and wanted. He used violence to make them obey. He threatened to hurt someone they loved if they told. He used drugs to coerce them into doing things they would never do willingly. Alex noticed, studied, and flattered his victims into psychological slavery so they could be used and discarded like common pieces of garbage. It takes malice to do this. It takes methodical, repetitive, premeditated, and intentional malice to abuse others in this way. This kind of malice happens in marriages and homes every day.

Macy's story isn't unlike the story of any other victim of abuse. No woman signs up for a life of violence, fear, and control. No woman wants to be used, abused, or discarded. No woman wants to become drug addicted to soothe the pain. Women in abusive relationships feel trapped, enslaved, forced, and without a will or a way out. They love the good they see in their partners. They love the way their partners made them feel special in the beginning. They unwittingly believe that things will get better if they just figure out how to make their abusers happy. They believe that things will go back to the way they were when they first met.

Shannon's Story

Shannon met Derik through a mutual friend. Shannon was a graduate student studying social work and Derik was a youth pastor at an area church. Derik was from the East Coast, new to his position, and eager to get to know Shannon. He showed interest in her right away. Shannon was a good listener with a big heart who felt flattered when Derik showed her so much attention.

Her dad was a pastor but was always involved with church duties. She doubted her dad even remembered her birthday unless he was reminded by her mom or his secretary. He never really paid attention to her, except for what she could do for the church. Shannon didn't blame him. He was working for God, after all. She just figured she wasn't interesting enough to catch his attention. That's why Shannon felt so good when Derik noticed her. He was tall and strong, with a devilish charisma. Sometimes he would say off-color things to get a laugh, or make fun of the overweight kids in his youth group with his friends. But all his friends would laugh, so she thought this was a normal way youth pastors blew off steam.

As Shannon and Derik continued dating, Derik expressed disappointment with Shannon's friends and any extracurricular activities that took her away from him. She limited her extra time so she could be there for Derik more often. As her world shrank, his entitlement to her grew. Coming over from her internship one day, she walked into Derik's apartment, filled with his friends. They were laughing about Derik's close calls with the Highway Patrol. Derik was bragging about how he could smooth talk a policeman out of giving him a ticket. Shannon, wanting to join in on the fun, jokingly interrupted, "Not last time! Let me remind you that just two weeks ago, you got pulled over by a female cop, and she gave you a ticket for speeding!"

All the guys in the room laughed at Derik being put in his place, but Derik's face went white, and his eyes went black. Shannon knew she'd said too much, that she'd crossed the line. She didn't mean for Derik to get laughed at. She thought she was just being funny.

Later that night, after his friends had all gone home, Derik took Shannon's arms in his hands and squeezed them so hard so she couldn't move. He drew her close, breathed down her neck and threatened that if she ever publicly humiliated him again, she would know what real public humiliation felt like. She thought he might break her forearms with his pressure, but he released her with a shove against the wall. She was speechless and terrified. He strode into the kitchen, put on an apron, and said with a smile, "Now, what shall we make for dinner?"

The violence increased over time to include shoving her into walls, slamming her head against her desk, and deleting her class papers right before the due date. After his violent rage subsided, he would cradle Shannon's bandaged head and ask for forgiveness. He would say that he just couldn't stand to lose her, that he needed her so desperately, he felt crazy when she went against him or away from him. He told her he loved her so much, it made him snap, and he just couldn't control himself.

Rachel, Macy, and Shannon's stories are just a few examples of the tactics Abusers use to lure and keep their partners, and how victims fall prey to their Abusers. Now let's look at the nature of abuse. As in the case of Macy, the abuse was not limited to physical violence. Abuse never is. You may automatically think of abuse as being physical in nature, and you would be right in thinking so. However physical violence never happens by itself; it occurs with various other abuses such as emotional, psychological, sexual, and financial. What's more, women in verbally hostile and emotionally ravaging relationships are still experiencing abuse, albeit without physical violence.

What Is Considered Abuse? What Is "Domestic Violence"?

Emotional Abuse

- Calling a partner degrading names like fat, ugly, stupid, crazy, sensitive, or lazy
- Controlling a partner's everyday life (taking her keys, monitoring her phone, locking doors, reading her emails, taking away special items)
- Preventing a partner from talking to people who can help (doctors, counselors, pastors)
- Humiliating a partner in public or when they're with friends and family
- Manipulating a partner with threats, lies, misplaced blame, and guilt
- Being jealous and isolating a partner from friends and family
- Acting in ways that make a partner feel afraid

Psychological Abuse

- Brainwashing a partner or trying to make them confused about reality; "crazy-making," or gaslighting
- Secretly monitoring a partner through technology or other means so that the abuser seems to have omnipresence and know everything about a partner

- Forcing a partner to stay awake for long hours leading to chronic exhaustion
- Using religion or another belief system to promote or defend abusive behavior
- Forcing children to engage in verbal or physical abuse of a partner
- Threatening to "out" a partner regarding private matters
- Threatening to have a partner deported if she is undocumented
- Switching from violent behavior to kind behavior in order to regain trust of a partner (and ultimately power and control over a partner)

Economic Abuse

- Controlling the family money
- Keeping account access for himself
- Forcing a partner to give her paychecks to him
- Not allowing a partner to work, go to school, or attend other activities that would promote economic independence
- Depriving a partner of money to pay for basic expenses, such as for personal hygiene items
- Trying to get a partner fired from work by calling repeatedly, showing up, or starting conflict with his partner's coworkers
- Taking away a partner's passport, social security card, driver's license, or other documents so she is unable to establish independence, financial or otherwise

Sexual Abuse

- Causing a partner to be hurt during sex
- Forcing a partner to perform sexual acts
- Having affairs outside of their relationship

- Forcing a partner to have sex with other people for money
- Purposely infecting a partner with HIV/AIDS or a sexually transmitted illness (STI)

Physical Abuse

- Pinching, poking, slapping, biting, pushing, punching, strangling, burning, or cutting (etc.) a partner
- Forcing a partner to take drugs
- Hurting a partner's pet
- Taking away a partner's assistance devices, such as glasses, hearing aid, walking aids

Qualities and Characteristics of the Abuser

- **Narcissistic:** You, the children, and the world revolve around the Abuser and his needs and moods. The Abuser feels powerful and elated when people walk on eggshells around him.
- **Jealous and Possessive:** He may accuse you of constantly flirting or being secretively attracted to other men. "I saw the way you looked at him; don't try to deny that you have a thing for him. You're lying!"
- **Disarming:** The Abuser can be so charming, flattering, or charismatic that people are often distracted from seeing his alarming character flaws.
- **Moody:** The Abuser can appear happy and gregarious one minute, and then suddenly triggered to hot rage or cold aloofness the next. His moods are unstable, inconsistent, unpredictable, and he's easily frustrated.
- **Isolating:** The Abuser may complain about close friends or family to the point of forbidding you from seeing them,

saying, "Your family are troublemakers, always getting in our business. I don't want you going over there anymore."

- **Controlling:** Using manipulation, guilt, coercion, and threats, the Abuser will control your finances, your time with friends, your job, your family, and your comings and goings. If your activities do not fit his purposes, those activities must stop. His controlling nature is cleverly disguised as concern and protection for you.

- **Critical:** The Abuser regularly criticizes others' appearance, ability, economic status, or morality. "She is so ugly/fat/dumb; I can't believe anybody likes her," or "He calls himself a Christian, but he is really just self-righteous."

- **Disrespectful:** Not sparing his own family, the Abuser will say disrespectful, inappropriate, and degrading things to and about his own mother and/or sisters.

- **Duplicitous:** The Abuser acts kindhearted and caring in public or when others are watching, and then intimidating and angry behind closed doors.

- **Superior:** Not believing that you are his equal, the Abuser expects you to carry out his orders, meet his every need, and behave perfectly according to his ever-changing standards. Believing you are inferior in looks, strength, intelligence, and ability, his way is always right.

- **Disingenuous:** When apologizing, the Abuser chooses words that sound good, but his tone and demeanor tell you he doesn't really regret his actions. He may say that he won't behave abusively again, but he makes no significant or meaningful effort to change, seek help, or live differently.

- **Cruel:** Inflicting harm on others through words or deeds energizes the Abuser and makes him feel powerful. This insatiable need for power trumps any sense of morality, guilt, or conscience.

I call this type of person the Abuser to help with understanding and instruction, but I do not believe that Losers, Users, and Abusers have fixed labels for a lifetime. Any person can change, heal, and grow if and when he wants to badly enough. I use these labels to help you categorize your relationship and your partner. But that categorization is just a starting point. Moving from toxicity to health is a long, arduous process of quarantine, surgery, recovery, and stabilization. It cannot be forced, rushed, or court-ordered. It must be surrendered into the hands of helpers, physicians, professionals, interventionists, and, ultimately, the hands of God. Without God's healing power, the poison in a person and in a relationship *will not* heal.

The fatal flaw is not only present inside the Abuser, it is inside of you as well. You are not responsible for the abuse, or his cruel treatment, or his anger. However, your fatal flaw is believing that it's your job to help him, fix him, and love him the way he needs, so that he can get better. You believe you must protect him. At your core, you believe you are worth less than true love; your real value is to keep him together. But you are wrong.

This faulty belief has grave consequences to you, your children, and even your Abuser. No matter how you've been treated in your past, or what degrading childhood traumas informed your sense of self, or what controlling relationships you've endured, or how he has brainwashed you into thinking you're nothing, *you deserve love.* You deserve respect. Submitting your faulty beliefs into the loving hands of God will help you realize that you are worthy of being seen, known, and unconditionally accepted.

How it Feels to Be in a Relationship with an Abuser

Your feelings are your friend. They are informants to your body and brain so they can know to take action. Women who've lived with abuse in their home often stop listening to their feelings because either they are too painful or sharing them may cause trouble. However, learning to listen to your feelings again can help you decide your next steps. Women in abusive relationships will feel:

- **Hypervigilant**: You may feel an increased responsiveness to stimuli (knock at the door, car braking, sound of his car in the driveway). You tend to automatically scan your environment for threats.

- **On high alert to his moods**: You read your partner's facial expressions, vocal tones, and body language for hints at his mood in case you are required to deflect, intervene, appease, or escape.

- **Preoccupied with his happiness**: Even when your partner is away, you are constantly thinking of ways to make him happy or to ease his pain. You desperately want him to be pleased with you, your cooking, your housecleaning, your child raising, etc., and feel responsible for his negative feelings about these things.

- **Confused**: You find it difficult to be sure what is true about your partner. You wonder which of his incongruent behaviors you can trust—the nice side or the mean side? The caring side or the cruel side?

- **A lost sense of self**: You become so preoccupied with your partner's life, moods, and behaviors, you stop thinking about yourself and your own needs. You find yourself constantly trying to protect your kids from him, and him from himself; you have no energy or will to take care of your true needs.

- **Controlled**: Either by actions, threats of action, or oppressive dominance, you feel trapped, smothered, and suffocated. You feel like you have no options and like you are powerless to make things better. You feel watched, imprisoned, and alone.

- **Eventual emotional detachment**: Once oppressiveness takes its toll, your feelings for your partner grow cold. You may feel numb, like a half-dead person just trying to exist. You detach emotionally from your partner because the hot/cold/repeat cycle has worn you thin. You may no longer love him; you just don't know how to leave him.

- **Conflicted and afraid**: You constantly weigh the pros and cons of whether to leave or stay. You are afraid that his abuse will worsen if you distance yourself from him. But if you stay and pretend nothing is wrong, you are afraid he may kill you. "Kill" means to die physically, but to be sure, you may already feel dead emotionally.

- **Dread**: You fear that his treatment of you and/or your children will only get worse over time, and that you are powerless to change it.

I've worked with Abusers before who say, "Oh, I'd never really hurt my wife. Sometimes things get out of hand. But my bark is worse than my bite." But when interviewing the wives, they report feeling quite differently. Partners of men who abuse report feeling so afraid of their partner's rage, they wonder if it may explode to something worse. The rage itself feels so threatening, they have the same physiological response as they would to actually being hurt or killed.

Why Are We Attracted to Abusers?

The Bad Boy Syndrome

There are countless magazine articles, talk show interviews, and coffee shop conversations deliberating why women are attracted to the Bad Boy persona. Many say that women's caretaking nature is piqued when they encounter someone "hard to love." Perhaps the nurturing nature in women needs to reach the unreachable or love the unlovable. Others say that the Bad Boy represents a challenge to women and "fixing" him would be a great ego boost.

This phenomenon is explained best this way. The Bad Boy is a symbol of all that primitive women would find attractive: strength, virility, self-reliance, competitiveness, and confidence. All these characteristics, at first glance, would make him a good catch, with the ability to protect, provide, and carry on the species. In fact, if the Bad Boy sets his attentions on you, you may find it difficult to resist. It feels flattering, ego-boosting, and sexually stimulating. The sex appeal can be astonishingly strong. There is something thrilling about getting the manliest, or macho-est (is that a word?), or smartest, or richest man in the room to take notice of little-ole-you. There is nothing wrong, sick, or misplaced about being attracted to a Bad Boy. However, to pursue him with hopes of making him truly love you is just north of crazy. He does not love. He possesses.

The Bad Boy is much more serious than a simple "persona" when we are talking about real abuse, real violence, and real psychological damage. If we dig a little deeper into the Bad Boy persona, we may very well find the Abuser. It's one thing to be attracted to an Abuser; it's another thing to fall in love with one, expecting to be loved back.

Simply put, it is natural to be attracted to the Bad Boy. But it is sick to fall in love with him. There is something sick inside you, in the Soul Hole left from previous traumas, that makes the Abuser irresistible. His selfish nature draws you to him like a polar magnet. Even though your head, your friends, and your family may be telling you, "He's not good for you," you fall for him anyway. It feels impossible to say "no" to his pull.

The Snake

Remember the man-cub Mowgli in the Disney classic, *The Jungle Book*? Mowgli was a sweet, innocent boy, all alone in the world and down on his luck, when Kaa the snake just happened along. Disguising himself as a helpful friend, Kaa lured Mowgli into an unconscious slumber with the hypnotic power of his googly gaze. The same thing happens to women everywhere, myself included. Although inner alarm systems warned me that things seemed a little "off," I've trusted a Snake before. The promises were a direct hit, the sales pitch pitch-perfect, and the lies tasted so sweet, I just wanted more. Then the Snake showed himself for what he was, and I regretted the day I ever met him.

The Snake has an uncanny ability to hide his true self and intentions, making him seem like something he is not. All the while, you are being hunted. This process may feel like being romantically pursued or the object of his desire, or even the apple of his eye. But make no mistake: *he* sees you as prey to be controlled and ultimately consumed. He is unable to connect, to feel, or to have intimacy because reptiles don't even have the brain capacity to do that! Reptiles don't stay in pods, or flocks, or herds. No! They live cold-blooded, slithering, loner lives, hunting and consuming prey. They are great for insect and rodent population control, but not for tenderhearted relationships. The trouble is, you won't know he is a Snake until you get too close. You thought he was intellectual, superior, self-controlled, and poised. You didn't know he was poised to strike. Until he strikes you.

Convincing Groupies

Oftentimes, the Abuser will keep other respectable-looking people around him, lending to his credibility and trustworthiness. I call them Groupies. Others have called them Apaths. Apaths collude with the Abuser, willingly blinded to his malice.[29] A friend of mine, unfortunately, got up close and personal with a Groupie-protected Abuser. She was a well-educated, well-intentioned women's pastor who partnered in various projects with another organization and pastor named Frank. Frank was surrounded by other pastors and missionaries. By all outward appearances, this gifted speaker seemed like a legitimate Christian minister. Once my friend started working with Frank, however, she discovered him to be moody, angry, controlling, and secretive. The more she snooped, the more secrets she uncovered. It turns out that he and his groupies all had some kind of sexual impropriety in their past. One had been convicted of incest, one had prior charges brought against him that were dismissed, and one was estranged from her children because of she had neglected to report their abuse from a past boyfriend.

The more my friend got to know them, she learned they all viewed themselves as victims of society, their bitter exes, or their "vindictive" adult children. They had created an alternate reality where they were

---

29 McGregor and McGregor, *The Empathy Trap.*

the good ones, the special ones. They were all willing to vouch for the Head Abuser, Frank, to do whatever he asked them to do, to keep him feeling untouchable. All had some personal interest in colluding with him on his budding "ministry" empire and were willing to let him do whatever it took to get there, even if it meant stepping on people who got in the way. It was the sickest form of "Christian ministry" she had personally experienced. After seeing clearly through all the smoke and mirrors, she cut all ties with their organization, even though it cost her a lot of time and money to do so.

After parting ways, she complained, "How could I have gotten so involved with them? Why didn't I see the red flags earlier?" If you've ever left a psychologically manipulative relationship, you probably asked yourself the same questions. Please, don't beat yourself up. Your Abuser, whether emotionally, physically or psychologically, did enough of that already.

No wonder it is difficult to see an Abuser's true identity; he keeps other seemingly "good" people around, making him look good. People fall prey to this kind of Abuser because they believe the convincing lies the Abuser and his groupies are living.

You Have a Dream

Another reason you may be attracted to Abusers, is that you have a dream of it all working out. You want to look past the bad so you can keep the image of what he could become always in your mind. You overlook bullying, badgering, threats, and domination to keep your dream alive that someday your Abuser will turn into the man he was destined to be. You are the only one who believes in him, the only one who can see past the jerk on the outside to see the hurting boy on the inside. You hold the dream for both of you, and you'd rather die than give it up. I hope it never comes to that. Your fantasy can never be reality if hopes and dreams are your only commodity.

No One Showed You What True Love Is

Your backstory may be different from everybody else's, but there is one thing you have in common with every woman who has ever loved the Abuser: you thought you could get something from him that you couldn't get for yourself—whether it be love, affirmation, validation, promotion, acceptance, or just to feel special. You believed that he could fill the hole, meet the need, or be the miracle you wanted all your life.

The reason your radar didn't go off like everyone else's did is because you're deaf. Someone in your past dulled your senses to the point that you can't recognize abuse for what it is. Maybe it was your father who only shared emotion in angry outbursts about the way you dressed, or talked, or picked your friends. Maybe it was your mother who criticized you in public for being too skinny. Maybe your father was unavailable or disinterested, sending you the unspoken message, "You're not important enough to keep my attention." These are original abuses from original Abusers.

When we are trained to overlook judgmental criticisms, emotionally abusive manipulation, shame-filled accusations, or denial of hurting hearts, we become deaf to what should alarm us. Hurting others without apology should alarm us. Name-calling and lewd talk should alarm us. Duplicitous, dishonest behavior should alarm us. Manipulating with guilt and shame should alarm us. Possessive, controlling jealousy should alarm us. But they don't because we grew up with them as normal ways of family interaction. We are deaf to our inner alarm system.

The hope and promise of getting the unloving person to love us, the abandoning person to stay, or the egomaniac to think we're special is so alluring that it's a deafening noise compared to any weak danger signals going off.

When we've been trained to excuse another's bad behavior all our lives, it is unbelievably easy to excuse the dark side of the Abuser. You may excuse the Abuser as naturally and automatically as brewing your coffee in the morning. It's never occurred to you to do otherwise.

Though the Abuser doesn't look, sound, or seem like the original Abuser at first glance, the dynamic—oh, that deadly dynamic—is hauntingly familiar. It's the exhilaration of being *seen*, after a lifetime of being ignored. It's the thrill of being *special*, when you're used to being common. Or the promise of being truly *known*, when you've felt misjudged and misunderstood for so long. The holes made by your original abusers are a chasm left wanting, desperate, and aching. So, you mistakenly look to another Abuser to fill the hole your original abuser could never fill.

But He Looked So Perfect at First

Women often tell me that they never saw it coming. They never suspected the man they loved would end up being abusive, unfaithful, or wholly self-centered. One reason women don't suspect the Abuser's true intentions is because the Abuser is highly skilled at creating false personas.

I often wonder if the Abusers I've worked with actually believe the lies they spin. Many have deluded themselves to the point they can no longer tell fact from fiction, reality from the fantasy they've created in their heads. They are master spinners of truth, often craftily mixing things you know to be true with things you're unsure of, until you push past reason and logic in order to believe whatever they say, hook, line, and sinker. You *want* to believe that their incredible lies are true, and so you do.

The bible talks about these kind of people as being "darkened in their understanding, alienated from the life of God because of the ignorance that is in them, due to their hardness of heart." [30]

And "…since they did not think it worthwhile to retain the knowledge of God, he gave them over to a depraved mind, to do what ought not to be done. They have become filled with every kind of wickedness, evil, greed and depravity. They are full of envy, murder, strife, deceit and malice. They are gossips, slanderers, God-haters, insolent, arrogant and boastful; they invent ways of doing evil; they disobey their parents; they are senseless, faithless, heartless, ruthless. Although they know God's righteous decree that those who do such things deserve death, they not only continue to do these very things but also approve of those who practice them."[31]

Pathological lying is a skill. They practice until it's nearly impossible to tell the fraudulent from the real. Everything looks right and sounds right, even though it may not *feel* right. That is why it is important to hear and to trust the uneasy, slimy feeling you get when something looks too good to be true. If you hang around something slimy for too long, you *will* get slimed.

The following is a diagram that explains the inner motivations of Abusers and the Bonded Victims they marry. You'll see that fear drives the Abuser/Bonded-Victim relationship, ultimately resulting in feelings of insignificance and rejection.

---

30 Eph 4:18 (English Standard Version).
31 Rom 1:28-32 (New International Version).

Abuser and Bonded Victim Paradigm[32]

Abuser Paradigm	Bonded Victim Paradigm	Healthy Paradigm
Fear of insignificance—My greatest fear is "not mattering."	*Fear of Dying*—My greatest fear is being abandoned or harmed by the one I love.	*Love*—True love casts out all fear. I am loved and safe in God's hands.
Competition—I must compare, compete, and dominate to feel worthwhile.	*Competition*—I must compare, compete, and morph into what he wants in order to feel love.	*Self-Acceptance*—I offer myself love, forgiveness, and help. I stay away from "one-up, one-down" relationships.
Ownership—I see people as objects to own and control for my desires.	*Slavery*—I am not my own; I belong to him. He controls me.	*Freedom*—I am free to make choices without fear of rejection, abandonment, or punishment.
Socio-pathology—I create a fantasy where I make the rules and I am not accountable.	*Denial*—In order to survive, I normalize the abuse and pathology in my relationship.	*Reality*—Seeing through deception and malice, I see the world as it really is. I can see what is true.
Shame—Secretly, I feel disgusting, but I project it onto others so others won't see me this way.	*Shame*—I feel unworthy of real love. I am ashamed of what I've become.	*Grace*—I am unbound by shame and free to offer love to self and others.
Attack and Abuse—Blaming, manipulating, and violating others makes me feel good and powerful.	*Bonded Victim*—Through traumatizing events, I become more attached to my abuser than ever.	*Boundaries*—I recognize my own needs and value and attract others who do the same.
Isolation—My pathological behaviors has distanced me from relationship.	*Isolation*—I become more and more lonely in the world I let him create for me.	*Belonging*—I have healthy bonds with caring people.
Insignificance—My pathological behaviors ultimately imprison or kill me, making me insufferably insignificant. My greatest fear has come true.	*Disappearance*—I slowly lose part of myself until I'm invisible, a living dead person. My greatest fear has come true.	*Significance*—I know that I matter to God, myself, and other people. I keep healthy people in my life.

---

32 Idolatry used here means to worship someone or something other than God. When we honor God above others, then we agree with God's natural order of things. We see people as equals, not greater or less than ourselves. We have reasonable expectations of others and ourselves, and see God as a Source of life instead of others.

166

Is it Possible to Turn Abusers into Lovers?

Anything is possible with the Love of God, but usually Abusers don't want to change. Manipulative, abusive, and pathological people can come to forgiveness in Christ, but they may never be fit for a marriage relationship in their lifetime. I do not believe that becoming a Christian, repenting of sins, or even staying in recovery programs will make the Abuser suited for intimate relationships. Like an alcoholic avoiding bars to stay sober, an abusive person who is serious about life change would do well to avoid intimate romantic relationships for a good long while—possibly years. A sign of true healing may very well be a commitment to stay single. The thing that is required for authentic change, is the very thing Abusers refuse to give up— their ego. For an Abuser to truly change, he would have to let go of his self-obsessed, control-starved, manipulating ego, and this is often too much of a sacrifice for an Abuser to make.

Is it possible to turn Abusers into Lovers? Maybe this is the wrong question to ask, because it's "him-focused." You may be better off asking yourself,

"Is it possible for me to heal and receive true love?"

This question is within your power to answer, and is "you-focused." Only you are responsible for you, and your Abuser is responsible for himself, although he'd like you to believe otherwise. If you are waiting for your Abuser to change so that you can finally feel loved, you are waiting for the wrong thing. You must first love yourself enough to get safe. If your Abuser is going to do any changing at all, you must remove yourself from the path by which his change can happen. His healing will not come through you; it must come through God. Your being in an unsafe, physically, and/or emotionally abusive environment will only prolong and prevent significant change.

Is it possible for Abusers to change? Yes, but it's not your job to do it, orchestrate it, beg for it, make the appointment for it, or even pray for it. This is God's job. Only He can heal what is broken, clean what is toxic, and set right what is wrong. Helping your Abuser is not your responsibility. It's your job to get safe. That's it. Your prayers are better spent asking God to help you get and stay psychologically, emotionally, and physically safe.

* *

It's your job to get safe. That's it.

* *

You may fear that if you leave, you will lose any link you have to him, or that he will walk away forever, and that you are the only thing keeping yourself together. You must face this fear and commit it to God. Your Abuser can never make you whole. You must be willing to walk away from him and his abuse for you to ever heal and experience true love.

On the other hand, you may fear that if you leave, you will only aggravate him to the point of doing more harm, becoming more dangerous, or seeking revenge. *This is a valid fear.* Women are at an increased risk of harm shortly after separation from an abusive partner.[33] **Leaving a vindictive Abuser demands caution and outside assistance.** Important Steps to Leaving an Abuser follow in the next section.

---

33 Ronet Bachman and Linda E. Saltzman, *Violence Against Women: Estimates From the Redesigned Survey* 1, Bureau of Justice Statistics (January 2000).

Steps to Living in the Pink

You must take brave steps to find safety and separation from the relationship abuse you are experiencing. Nothing will ever get better if you don't take this necessary step. You cannot heal if you are in an abusive relationship. You cannot recover if you are drowning in toxic waste. You can never thrive If you are just trying to survive. You must get distance, space, and time to think clearly without threat or pressure. Many battered women agree that the peaceful freedom of getting away from their abuser is worth the painful and frightening steps to leave. But the timing is up to you. You are the best judge of when it is time to go.

Steps to Leaving an Abusive Relationship: Leaving is often a gut-wrenching decision fraught with uncertainty and fear. Many women want to hold on to the relationship because they fear what could happen to them if they leave. Leaving is often a last ditch, life or death effort to save themselves and/or their children. She knows that his abusive, controlling, and threatening behavior will worsen if she tries to leave, so she stays to stay alive, to be the buffer for her kids, or to try to get back to normal. But life can never be normal with an Abuser.

If women don't feel as though their lives are physically threatened, they certainly feel as though their livelihood is. Women in abusive relationships fear losing their children, losing their home, losing all they hold dear. Often, they feel as though they must choose between living and dying—if it's not physical death, then emotional. Many will leave abusive relationships repeatedly, only to go back because of the Abuser's pleading, badgering, empty promises, or threats. Sometimes women return to their abuser because they feel they and their children have nowhere else to turn.

Leaving abusive relationships is extremely risky and should never be considered lightly. Researchers Gottman and Jacobson write, "No matter how careful the plan to ensure escape, no matter how expert the advice, no one can predict with anything close to certainty how a batterer will respond."[34] You won't know if your Abuser will let go and move on, or lash out with threatening violence or deadly intent. You are the best judge of when you are ready to leave. One thing is for certain, you cannot guarantee your safety if you stay.

Considerations: If you are in an abusive relationship, you should consider both your short-term and long-term needs. Consider assistance programs that focus on the critical days after leaving. Talk with friends or family about a temporary situation where you can get needed space and separation. An assistance program will include shelter, safety, and guidance at the time you may be most at risk for your Abuser's retribution or your own temptation to return. Resources and contact information are at the back of this book.

Get Help: Next, you will need the assistance of many different resources. It is necessary to seek assistance from not only trusted friends and family, but from experts and organizations. The people from reputable domestic violence advocacy groups and shelters will listen to your unique situation and help you figure out a plan that will be best for you. Friends and family are certainly helpful support systems, but may not know how to expertly maneuver leaving an abusive situation. Family crisis centers or victim advocates can act as your link to the various health, legal, and social sectors that you'll need to get and stay on your feet.

---

34 John Gottman and Neil Jacobson, *When Men Batter Women* (New York: Simon and Schuster, 1998), 239.

Tell Trustworthy People: It is important to open up to several trusted individuals. If your family or friends are trustworthy, tell them what you've been going through behind closed doors. Some family or friends may be loyal to your Abuser and may be manipulated into betraying your confidence. Be careful who you tell—make sure they are trustworthy. The people in your life may not know how to protect or help you, but you must fight the misplaced shame you feel and come out of hiding. Your temptation to protect your Abuser's reputation must be put aside to make yourself safe. This is often the first step in healing. Some people may want you to leave right away, and understandably so. But they may not grasp the possible danger in your decision to leave or the delicacy and right timing you need to stay safe.

No Contact Orders: There are several laws and protections in place for victims of domestic violence. These options are designed to protect the victim from further abuse. They may not stop stalking, intimidation, or abuse from happening, but they do permit the victim to call the police and have the abuser arrested if the order is broken. An attorney should be consulted for your specific needs. In general, Domestic Violence Protection Orders, No Contact Orders and Restraining Orders, Move Out Provisions, or Peaceful Contact Protections can be issued depending on your state and what you need. Talking with an attorney will help you determine if one or any of these options is recommended for your personal situation.

Make a Safety Plan: Next you'll need a Safety Plan. This is often best carried out when you can collaborate with a trusted person to support you. The Safety Plan can include a memorized list of the phone numbers of trusted people, a few ways you have practiced escaping your home safely, a separate and private bank account and credit card, three or four options for places to go, and the ability to change your phone number. You will find a safety plan template at the end of this chapter.

Items You'll Need: You will need several items before you go, and if you can do so safely, try to collect them. Gathering important items makes leaving seem very real, so you may feel hesitant. Push through this uncomfortable reality. Consider bringing important papers and information with you, such as social security cards and birth certificates for you and your children, your marriage license, leases or deeds in your name or both yours and your partner's names, your checkbook, your charge cards, bank statements and charge account statements, insurance policies, proof of income for you and your spouse (pay stubs or W-2's), and any documentation of past incidents of abuse (photos, police reports, medical records, etc.).

After You Leave

The Abuser can make it very difficult or dangerous for a victim to find safety or leave a relationship. Some of their tactics can be repeated or intensified when a victim leaves. In fact, a victim's risk of getting killed by an Abuser greatly increases when she is in the process of leaving or has just left a relationship. Domestic violence advocates understand that being in an abusive relationship is hard and that leaving can be dangerous. When you feel the time is right, you can **call 1.800.799.SAFE (1.800.799.7233) to talk to a domestic violence advocate** about how you are feeling and what you need to stay safe. You do not have to face the violence of your Abuser alone.

How Do You Know if the Abuser Has Changed?

The best way to identify true healing and transformation is by evidence-based measures. The Abuser must be able to demonstrate measurable behaviors and patterns over a long period of time before you can properly build trust. If you don't see evidence of the Abuser changing for the better, then no matter what promises he makes, he has not changed and should not be trusted.

Evidence the Abuser is Changing for the Good

- He takes responsibility for *all* physical, sexual, emotional, economic, and psychological abuse against you.
- He honors your requests for space and boundaries fully without negotiating, complaining, badgering or manipulating for more out of you.
- He blames only himself for his abusive actions, expecting and asking nothing from you in return for his apology.
- He voluntarily participates in a recovery or counseling program for batterers.
- He voluntarily invites and accepts accountability from other sources besides you.
- There is regular communication between several sources besides yourself like counselors, prosecutors, and treatment advisors to help determine if he is "faking" good behavior or has a genuine interest in change.
- Time—a sufficient amount of time.

Evidence the Abuser Has NOT Sufficiently Changed

- He minimizes past abuse and makes excuses for it.
- He denies that his actions were serious, dangerous, and abusive.

- He blames his stress level, boss, family troubles, or you for his behavior.
- He pressures you to go to marriage counseling.
- He claims that you owe him.
- He makes threats that he'll hurt himself or you if you don't come back.
- He badgers you with phone calls or unwanted visits.
- He pressures you to make decisions about the relationship.
- He is demanding, caught in a lie, or is using drugs or alcohol.
- He uses your kids or family against you.

Positive signs of change are a good thing, but the progress doesn't obligate you to reconcile. You may still have months of healing and recovery to do yourself. Feeling pressured to rush this process will only cause trouble down the road. Take time to slowly move through the steps of healing for yourself before you consider any decisions to reconcile. Time alone does not heal all wounds, but time is necessary for you to see consistent improvements, repentance, and sustained behavior change.

No matter the changes you see in your partner, how committed he is to recovery, or what spiritual transformation he has undergone, you may not *ever* feel safe around him. That is okay. Don't be guilted, manipulated, or coerced into reconciling with him if you have uneasy feelings. Remember, you are trying to recognize and prioritize your inner warning system. You had it turned on mute for so long, you couldn't hear it screaming at you. But now you are better at listening to it. If it is talking to you, cautioning you, then by all means, LISTEN! Do not force yourself to reengage with your partner if you have misgivings, unsettled feelings, or doubts. These feelings are to be recognized, not minimized. You are under NO obligation to ever return or reconcile, no matter what anyone says, preaches, or teaches.

Some Christian women mistakenly believe that their faith dictates to them that they *must* reconcile, if at all possible. They mistakenly believe that they are "not giving God a chance to heal their relationship" or "not prioritizing the marriage." They think they should work harder, try harder, and pray harder to have feelings for their partner again. They believe that since they promised to always love and honor their husbands, they are required by God to go back.

God made divorce available for people like you who cannot, and should not, live in psychologically and/or physically abusive relationships any longer, who should not bear the burden of cruelty, the sickness of wickedness, or the curse of manipulation any more. He gave you the *gift* of divorce so you can be free. If you don't want to reconcile, don't.

· ·

You must forgive your partner, because that frees you,
but you never have to get back together. Ever.

· ·

God Is on the Side of the Oppressed

God is always on the side of the oppressed. The following scriptures describe how God feels about this:

"LORD, You have heard the desire of the humble; You will pre-pare their heart; You will cause Your ear to hear, To do justice to the fatherless and the oppressed, That the man of the earth may oppress no more." [35]

---

35 Ps 10:14-18 (New King James Version)

"God's a safe-house for the battered, a sanctuary during bad times." [36]

"The Lord detests differing weights, and dishonest scales do not please him." [37]

"Start each day dealing with justice. Rescue victims from their exploiters." [38]

Even if your partner is in counseling or a program for batterers, there is no guarantee that he'll change. Many Abusers who go through counseling continue to be violent, abusive, and controlling. You must make your decision based on who he is now, not the man you hope he will become.

Once you are safe and relatively settled, use the following REPS for healing.

R Restore Order through Boundaries

Your life may feel disorganized, chaotic, and unsettled for a while. That's okay. Change is always messy and never goes as smoothly as we think it should. Expect many challenges along the way to your full recovery and healing. One way to mitigate those challenges is to pencil some boundaries into your life and calendar.

- **Limit unnecessary responsibilities**. Have you ever thought about what a body does when it's in survival mode? It shuts down the nonessential parts of the body and sends all its blood flow to the vital organs. The brain, the heart, and the lungs get the limited resources during a time of physical crisis. Give

---

36 Ps 9:9-10 (The Message).
37 Pr 20:23 (New International Version).
38 Jeremiah 21:12 (The Message)

yourself permission to shut down the nonessentials of life so you can keep the main things functioning. Your vital organs should be **Safety, Shelter, and Provision**. You can put the other responsibilities in your life on the shelf until you are out of crisis mode.

- **Limit mental drains.** Worrying, mind reading, analyzing, fortune-telling, and regretting the past are all internal pastimes that steal important energy. Worrying about the things you have no control over is a terrible way to spend your precious time. Give yourself a little time each day to worry, and when that time is up, tell yourself that you will worry again tomorrow, but that you're all done for today.

- **Limit negativity**. What you are going through is hard enough; you don't need additional negative stimulus to bring you down. Negative stimulus comes in the form of complaining, criticizing, judgmental talk, put-downs, mean jokes, sarcasm, and cynicism. Negative stimulus gives nothing to your life. You can do without it. Put boundaries around what you watch, read, listen to, and who you hang around. Positive influences, even if they're borderline cheesy, give life instead of stealing it.

- **Safety Plan:** See the end of this chapter for your personal safety plan. Your number one priority is you and your children's safety. As you work through your own safety plan, you will start to feel more tangible power and motivation. You will start to see that you can and will make it without him.

E Experience God

You may feel like you've been living in such a topsy-turvy world lately, that you can't even think about God, let alone experience

Him. If religion has been used to control or oppress you, then religious things may seem repulsive. If so, start with things, people, and places that bring you peace and comfort. You don't have to have a name or definitive religion to experience the goodness of God and rest in His goodness.

Your stress and fear may be screaming so loudly, it's hard to hear God. Don't fret; let safe and loving people be Jesus to you for a while. Lean on the helpers who know what you're going through. Tell them your story, and let them affirm your decision to leave. Connect with other women through domestic violence support groups and be encouraged that you are not the only one suffering in this way. Read survivor stories that help you see that the season you are in now is temporary, and that you will get through it one day at a time.

Many women will tell me stories of how they broke free from their abusers through the timely intervention of God. Maybe a friend called or showed up at the right time. Maybe it's the counselor who sees the abuse for what it is and validates the woman's experiences as abusive. Maybe it's a pastor, an attorney, or a TED talk that changes everything for you. I get to hear stories frequently of God's provision, enlightenment, and presence showing up at the right moment.

Prayer: When you are connected to a User or Abuser, you are not just connected with the person, you are connected to their darkness. Once you break it off with this person, you won't necessarily be free from their darkness. Prayer is an important way to push back this darkness with light. Ask your friends and family to regularly pray for your safety, your peace, and your provision. This threatening darkness can feel stifling, unsettling, and confounding. Prayer pushes it back and brings clarity and hope. If you don't know how to pray, here is an example:

"God, you have given me light and truth to see my situation. You can protect me and you can teach me how to protect myself. Put people in my life who will support me and advocate for me, and help me to advocate for myself. I am yours, and have nothing to fear. I trust you to promote justice, to provide for my needs, and to help me fully recover until I am whole again."

Church: Healthy churches value community and fellowship, and are free of manipulation and judgment. Church should be a place where you are seen, known, and unconditionally accepted. Healthy and caring churches are a place where you can find support in your faith, people who have been where you've been, and can offer encouragement. If you're in a church where you experience belittlement, shaming, sexism, or a beat down every week, consider finding a new church. Fast.

Church should also be a place where you can be safe from your User or Abuser. If he is trying to manipulate your church against you, encroach on your safe place, or intimidate you at church, you have the right to ask the church leadership to ask him to leave.

P Provide yourself with People

People who have never experienced psychological or physical abuse may not understand your struggles or your decisions. That's okay; they can't be expected to fully empathize. However, it is important to receive support from experts in the field who truly can empathize and advise. Community organizations, online communities, domestic violence agencies, women's support groups, victim advocacy groups, and savvy attorneys are examples of people who are trained to offer the right kind of support.

Many women will not feel right about sharing their dirty laundry with the church community because they don't want to spoil their partners' reputations. However, his reputation is not more valuable than your safety. Getting more people involved with your situation is the right thing to do. He most likely will try to limit your interaction with others, but this is exactly the wrong instinct. Inviting trustworthy individuals at church, such as a wise pastor who can see past the deception, is good and reasonable option. Remember, when the secret is exposed to the light, it loses its power. It is not your job to protect your partner. It's your job to receive the support you need.

Characteristics of Safe People

It's good to identify the characteristics safe people have in common so you recognize them when you see them. The Soul Holes that attracted you to your Loser, User, or Abuser may be attracting you to unsafe people in other areas of your life. Here are some telltale signs of people who are emotionally, physically, and psychologically safe to trust:

- They practice good boundaries by respecting your choices and opinions.
- They don't tell you what to do and how to do it.
- They don't give too much unwanted advice.
- They don't judge, look down upon, or tsk-tsk you for having challenges.
- They don't tell you that your relationship problems would go away if you would pray more, be more submissive, have more faith, or be a better Christian.
- They consider your wants, needs, and situation, letting you have the relational space you need.

- They don't treat you like a problem to be fixed or a project to manage; they know the difference between intimacy and enmeshment.
- They keep your private information private.
- They confront with compassion and gentleness, not criticism and judgment.
- They remain objective about your struggles and don't take sides or bash your partner.
- They respect your boundaries of space, time, and closeness.
- They practice good self-care.
- They can cope with unpleasant emotions or circumstances without lashing out, blaming, raging, or shutting down.
- They live authentically with their behaviors and actions, not just their words.
- They give grace toward weaknesses and imperfections.
- They don't have it all together. They are aware of their own imperfections, are familiar with their own pain, and have grown in recovery.

These characteristics are the result of God's intervention and healing. These are examples of the good fruit that is produced in a life that is emotionally healthy and growing. When you are looking for safe people with which to share your struggles and journey, consider these characteristics as a guide.

S Seek Intimacy with Self and God

I don't advise seeking intimacy with your partner. He is the last person with whom you want intimate contact. Seek to intimately know yourself and make yourself known with safe people. This takes time and should not be rushed. Slowly take an account of your own pain and your own experiences, being honest with yourself about the consequences of those experiences.

- **Ask God to help you be aware of your own value.** Accept yourself fully, just the way you are. *See* yourself as valuable, *know* yourself intimately, and *accept* yourself as fully human. Just human. Imperfectly perfect.
- **Be your own best friend.** Talk to yourself with respect and gentleness. Be kind to yourself. Let yourself off the hook. Give yourself credit for a job well done and forgiveness for the mistakes you have made.
- **Go back to the things you love.** Remember what it feels like to create, to dream, and to play. Get to know yourself again by reintroducing the things that bring you joy.
- **Invite healing.** Whether in the form of counseling or prayer or music or art, invite the healing that God is desperate to give you. Accept one small step at a time, into the fullness of your recovery. Often an expert in trauma recovery can help lead the way to your best self.

Women who suffer oppression and violence at the hands of someone they love need time, space, and support to take the necessary steps toward freedom and healing. Each woman must determine her own readiness—the point at which she declares, "No more. Never again." After making this decision, many of my clients will reflect on their pasts and see how God provided for them when they were destitute, how He guided them at a crossroads decision, and how He intervened when they needed Him most. Many couldn't see God's helping hands at the time, but, looking back, they recognize miracle after miracle.

You will see many miracles along your journey to healing too. But from where I stand, *you* are the true miracle. You can love and be loved. Your past abusive experiences have not ruled you out or deemed you unfit for happiness.

. . . .

Many couldn't see God's helping hands at the time, but, looking back, they recognize miracle after miracle.

. . . .

You want your love to be secure, unshakable, intimate, and passionate. This *is* possible! The next chapter is the Lovers Quadrant. You might expect the LOVERS Quadrant to be a happy, conflict-free, romantic nirvana—a perpetual date night of romantic bliss. You've seen the nightmare and now you want the dream! Is it possible? What does a healthy, happy relationship look like? What does it take to get it? These questions and more will be answered in the Lovers Quadrant.

YOUR PERSONAL SAFETY PLAN

Name: _____

Date: _____

The following steps are a plan for increasing my safety and preparing in advance for the possibility of violence. Although I do not have control over my partner's violence, I do have a choice about how to respond to him/her and how to best get myself and my children to safety.

STEP 1: Safety during a violent incident. Women cannot always avoid violent incidents. To increase safety, battered women use a variety of strategies.

I can use some of the following strategies:

A. If I decide to leave, I will _____ _____. (Practice how to get out safely. What doors, windows, elevators, stairwells, or fire escapes would you use?)

B. I can keep my purse and car keys ready and put them _____ _____ (location) so I can leave quickly.

 C. I can tell _____ about the violence and request that she or he call the police if she or he hears suspicious noises coming from my house.

D. I can teach my children how to call 911 the telephone to contact the police, the fire department, and other emergency services.

E. I will use _____ as my code with my children or my friends so they can call for help.

F. If I have to leave my home, I will go to _____.
(Decide this even if you don't think there will be a next time.)

G. I can also teach some of these strategies to some or all of my children.

H. When I expect we're going to have an argument, I'll try to move to a place that is low risk, such as _____. (Try to avoid arguments in the bathroom, garage, kitchen, near weapons, or in rooms without access to an outside door.)

I. I will use my judgment and intuition. If the situation is very serious, I can give my partner what he/she wants to calm him/her down, before I try to leave.

STEP 2: Safety when preparing to leave. Abused women frequently leave the residence they share with their battering partner. Leaving must be done with a careful plan in order to increase safety. Batterers often strike back when they believe that a battered woman is leaving a relationship. The following strategies can be used:

A. I will leave money and an extra set of keys with _____ so I can leave quickly.

B. I will keep copies of important documents or keys at _____ _____.

C. I will open a savings account by _____, to increase my independence.

D. Other things I can do to increase my independence include:

_____

185

E. I can keep change for phone calls on me at all times. I understand that if I use my telephone credit card, the following month's phone bill will show my batterer the numbers I called after I left. To keep my phone communications confidential, I must either use coins, or I might ask to use a friend's phone card for a limited time when I first leave.

F. I will check with _____ and _____ to see who would let me stay with them or lend me some money.

G. I can leave extra clothes or money with _____.

H. I will sit down and review my safety plan every _____ in order to plan the safest way to leave the residence.

_____ (Domestic violence advocate or friend's name) has agreed to help me review this plan.

I. I will rehearse my escape plan and, as appropriate, practice it with my children.

STEP 3: Safety in my own residence. There are many things that a woman can do to increase her safety in her own residence. It may be impossible to do everything at once, but safety measures can be added step by step.

Safety measures I can use:

A. I can change the locks on my doors and windows as soon as possible.

B. I can replace wooden doors with steel/metal doors.

C. I can install security systems including additional locks, window bars, poles to wedge against doors, an electronic system, etc.

D. I can purchase rope ladders to be used for escape from second floor windows.

E. I can install smoke detectors and fire extinguishers for each floor of my house/apartment.

F. I can install an outside lighting system that activates when a person is close to the house.

G. I will teach my children how to call me or _____ (name of friend, etc.) if my partner takes the children.

H. I will tell the people who take care of my children which people have permission to pick up my children and that my partner is not permitted to do so. The people I will inform about pick-up permission include:

_____ (name of school)

_____ (name of babysitter)

_____ (name of teacher)

_____ (name of Sunday-school teacher)

_____ (name[s] of others)

_____

I. I can inform _____ (neighbor) and _____ _____ (friend) that my partner no longer resides with me and that they should call the police if he is observed near my residence.

STEP 4: Safety with an Order of Protection. Many batterers obey protection orders, but one can never be sure which violent partner will obey and which will violate protective orders. I recognize that I may need to ask the police and the courts to enforce my protective order.

The following are some steps I can take to help the enforcement of my protection order:

A. I will keep my protection order _____ (location). (Always keep it on or near your person. If you change purses, that's the first thing that should go in the new purse.)

B. I will give my protection order to police departments in the community where I work, in those communities where I visit friends or family, and in the community where I live.

C. Most counties and states have registries of protection orders that all police departments can call to confirm a protection order. I can check to make sure that my order is on the registry. The telephone numbers for the county and state registries of protection orders are: _____ (county) and _____ (state).

D. I will inform my employer; my minister, rabbi, etc.; my closest friend; and _____ that I have a protection order in effect.

E. If my partner destroys my protection order, I will get another copy from the clerk's office.

F. If the police do not help, I can contact an advocate or an attorney and file a complaint with the chief of the police department or the sheriff.

G. If my partner violates the protection order, I can call the police and report the violation, contact _____

STEP 5: Safety on the job and in public. Each battered woman must decide if and when she will tell others that her partner has battered her and that she may be at continued risk. Friends, family, and co-workers can help to protect women. Each woman should carefully consider which people to invite to help secure her safety.

I can do any or all of the following:

A. I can inform my boss, the security supervisor, and _____ _____ at work.

B. I can ask _____ to help me screen my telephone calls at work.

C. When leaving work, I can _____.

D. If I have a problem while driving home, I can _____ _____.

E. If I use public transit, I can _____ _____.

F. I will go to different grocery stores and shopping malls to conduct my business and shop at hours that are different from those I kept when residing with my battering partner.

G. I can use a different bank and go at hours that are different from those kept when residing with my battering partner.

STEP 6: Safety and drug or alcohol use. Most people in our culture use alcohol. Many use mood-altering drugs. Much of this is legal, although some is not. The legal outcomes of using illegal drugs can be very hard on battered women, may hurt her relationship with her children, and can put her at a disadvantage in other legal actions with her battering partner. Therefore, women should carefully consider the potential cost of the use of illegal drugs. Beyond this, the use of alcohol or other drugs can reduce a woman's awareness and ability to act quickly to protect herself from her battering partner. Furthermore, the use of alcohol or other drugs by the batterer may give him an excuse to use violence. Specific safety plans must be made concerning drugs or alcohol use.

If drug or alcohol use has occurred in my relationship with my battering partner, I can enhance my safety by some or all of the following:

A. If I am going to use, I will do so in a safe place and with people who understand the risk of violence and are committed to my safety.

B. If my partner is using, I can _____ and/or _____.

C. To safeguard my children I could _____

_____.

STEP 7: Safety and my emotional health. The experience of being battered and verbally degraded by partners is usually exhausting and emotionally draining. The process of building a new life takes courage and incredible energy.

To conserve my emotional energy and resources and to avoid hard emotional times, I can do some of the following:

A. If I feel down and am returning to a potentially abusive situation, I can _____

_____.

B. When I need to communicate with my partner in person or by telephone, I can _____

_____.

C. I will try to use "I can ..." statements with myself and be assertive with others.

D. I can tell myself, "_____

_____" whenever I feel others are trying to control or abuse me.

E. I can read _____

_____ to help me feel stronger.

F. I can call _____ and _____ for support.

G. I can attend workshops and support groups at the domestic violence program or _____ to gain support and strengthen relationships.

STEP 8: Items to take when leaving. When women leave partners, it is important to take certain items. Beyond this, women sometimes give an extra copy of papers and an extra set of clothing to a friend, just in case they need to leave quickly.

Money: Even if I never worked, I can take money from jointly held savings and checking accounts. If I do not take this money, he can legally take the money and close the accounts.

Items on the following lists with asterisks by them are the most important things to take with you. If there is time, the other items might be taken, or stored outside the home. These items might best be placed in one location, so that if you must leave in a hurry, you can grab them quickly.

When I leave, I should take: identification for myself, children's birth certificate(s), my birth certificate, Social Security cards, school and vaccination records, money, checkbook, credit cards, keys (house, office, and car), driver's license and registration, medications, copy of protection order, copy of No Contact order, welfare identification, work permits, green cards, passport(s), divorce papers, medical records for all family members, lease/rental agreement, house deed, mortgage payment book, bank books, insurance papers, address book, pictures, jewelry.

Numbers to know:

Police/sheriff's department (local)—911 or _____

Police/sheriff's department_____

Prosecutor's office _____

Battered women's program (local) _____

National Domestic Violence Hotline: 800-799-SAFE (7233)

County registry of protection orders _____

State registry of protection orders _____

I will keep this document in a safe place and out of the reach of my potential attacker.

Review date: _____

Chapter 7

LOVERS: What You Always Wanted, but Didn't Know How to Get

"They slipped briskly into an intimacy from which they never recovered."

—F. Scott Fitzgerald, *This Side of Paradise*

When you are getting ready for something big, like a first date, or a test, or a job interview, or an important presentation, what do you do? I mean, besides apply lipstick? I have a few rituals to which you may relate. I rehearse. I talk to myself. I change my outfit six times. I obsess about worst-case scenarios. I procrastinate on Facebook. I pray. I run to the toilet ... you know, stuff like that. Jesus was the same way before His important events too. Well, not *exactly* the same, except for the praying part. I don't know if He did *any* of the other things except the praying part.

Jesus prepared Himself for many important events by talking to His father. Maybe the most significant thing He prepared Himself for was His trial and crucifixion. The night before His crucifixion, Jesus asked God for something that might surprise you. He was leaving his

BFFs behind and prayed specifically for them. But what did Jesus ask God for on their behalf?

Let me set the stage. Jesus referred to God as "Abba" or "Daddy." They spent a lot of time together talking, sometimes for hours before anyone else woke up. In the bible, we read that He experienced a unity with God marked by peace, wisdom, and power. Jesus took the loving experience He had with Abba and shared it with other people. Jesus spent three years befriending, teaching, and commissioning the people that came to Him, and called them His friends. They lived together, worked together, ate together, and traveled together. They were tight.

If you were Jesus and you knew the next day you would die for your friends, what would you pray for? The night before He sacrificed his life for His friends, and ultimately humanity, Jesus asked God for *intimacy.*

"That they may be one as we are one: I in them and you in me. May they be brought to complete unity."[39]

Intimacy. Jesus asked God to bring them together and unite them in heart. Jesus asked Abba to unite his friends as He and God were united. Jesus knew what He was asking. He knew that this kind of unity would require vulnerability, humility, and understanding. It would require a God-type unconditional love that couldn't be achieved in and of itself.

"So that they may be one as we are one."[40]

We want that kind of intimacy too, don't we? We want to be known deeply, seen as valuable, and loved unconditionally. We want

---

39 Jn 17:22-23 (New International Version).
40 Jn 17:11 (New International Version).

to have that special someone who has access to the deepest parts of our hearts. We want to have the kind of peace that unity between friends or partners produces.

But if you are like me, as soon as you say you want these things, the truth hits you that it's going to take a sacrifice to get them. Something has to die. Something has to be laid down, submitted, and killed at the altar. That something usually has to do with my pride, my self-protection mechanisms, my ego, and my self-consciousness. I have to be willing to be completely exposed, arms open to the intimacy God has for me—intimacy with Him and intimacy with others.

"I in them and you in me. May they be brought to complete unity to let the world know that you sent me and have loved them even as you have loved me." [41]

I'm afraid. What if I give my all and get only a little in return? What if I expose everything I am, and I find it's just too much for others to take? What if I'm too needy, too self-absorbed, too weak, too snobby, too boring, or too annoying? What if my vulnerability proves too much for them to handle? What if it makes them run away?

"that they may have the full measure of my joy within them." [42]

What if I really show up to my relationships—I mean completely? I put my whole self out there, not holding anything back. All the shameful parts, and selfish parts, and corny parts, and—oh geez, what about the PMS parts? And that's just with my friends. What about intimacy with Mr. Dashing? What is that going to require of me? What of my failings, and personality deficiencies, and lack of

---

41 Jn 17:23 (New International Version).
42 Jn 17:13 (New International Version).

self-discipline, and inability to learn from my mistakes? What about when I lose my way, lose myself, and lose heart? What if I'm just too much to take? Too high maintenance and just not worth it? What if I try and I try, and still, I end up alone?

"All I have is yours, and all you have is mine."[43]

Once or twice a year, I have this recurring dream that Mr. Dashing is seeing someone else. She's prettier and smarter and impossibly perfect in every way. I find out about it, and his response is indifference. The other woman glowers with disdain and smirks in my direction. In my dream, Mr. Dashing turns his back on me and leaves me out of their tight connection. I'm wounded and incensed. I silently scream, "What about me? What about me? Don't you see me; I'm right here? Am I invisible?"

These silent screams are rooted in my past when "invisible" was exactly what I was. Due to unhappy circumstances and human failings, feeling invisible was a painful reality while I was growing up. My recurring nightmare is leftover residue from a scorched time long ago.

"In this world you will have trouble. But take heart! I have overcome the world."[44]

Sometimes in my dream, I become violent, and I try to shake and punch Mr. Dashing. He acts as if I'm a dying fly on a window sill. I'm nothing. I scrape his skin with my angry fingernails, and still, he remains unaffected. My tears mean nothing. My fight means nothing. He looks through me. My best effort to stand up

---

43 Jn 17:10 (New International Version).
44 Jn 16:33 (New International Version).

for myself is a pathetic, desperate act to avoid the inevitability of my total worthlessness.

"They will leave me all alone. Yet I am not alone, for my Father is with me." [45]

I usually wake up from this dream with feelings somewhere between dread and anger. Realizing that this dream represents feelings from my past, and not my current reality, I usually try to regain some self-control. But these kinds of dreams take an emotional toll.

Usually after one of these dreams, I'm coy with Mr. Dashing. "I'm mad at you because you cheated on me again last night."

He'll say, "Oh really? Who was it with this time?"

I'll say, "I don't know; some tramp you met at work."

He'll ask, "Was she hot or rich? Hopefully both."

Then I'll play punch him in the arm, and we'll hug. He'll say something sweet like, "Only a fool would cheat on you, and I'm no fool," and then reality replaces my unconscious manufactured dream story. Everything is better, because reality is better than my nightmare.

But my body and heart sometimes get triggered from the pain of the past. They still need a little convincing.

The dream has nothing to do with Mr. Dashing or some impossibly perfect tramp—*er, woman.* It has everything to do with how I see myself, and what I believe about myself deep down. Though I'm seen, known, and unconditionally accepted by God and many people around me, Mr. Dashing included, sometimes I just don't *feel* it all the way through. In my nightmare, I am compelled to *fight* to matter. I shout so someone will notice I exist. I hit and scratch so

---

45 Jn 16:32 (New International Version).

someone will see I'm in pain. On the outside I scream, "I'm some-body!!!" because inside, I still wonder.

"I have given them the glory that you gave me, that they may be one as we are one—I in them and you in me—so that they may be brought to complete unity."[46]

These compulsions are toxic residue from past experiences. We all have them. Soul Holes. My "fits" for feeling worthwhile show up in my dreams, but are showing up less in real life now. This is prog-ress—progress that is due to the sheer determination to conquer it. It's due to people of light who saw through my insecurities and chose to love me anyway. It's due to the story of Jesus, that somehow I'm worth His life, completely exposed, arms wide open. It's an answer to Jesus' last night of prayer:

"As the Father has loved me, so have I loved you. Now remain in my love."[47]

"Ask and you will receive, and your joy will be complete."[48]

This mystery of doing everything backwards to go forwards is just so … *Jesus.* Shed light on the things you want to hide. Give away what you protect the most. Open up what you shut down Turn towards, not away.

Remaining in God's constant love enables us to sacrifice all, with no guarantees of our partner's love and acceptance in return. Even if the worst happens, and we are rejected by those we love, God is always with us and for us.

---

46 Jn 17:23 (New International Version).
47 Jn 15:9 (New International Version).
48 Jn 16:24 (New International Version).

"Then the world will know that you sent me and have loved them even as you have loved me."

The Lovers Quadrant is much better than fantasy—it's reality. The Lovers Quadrant is the space where two people are truly seen, known, and experience unconditional authentic love. It's what Jesus prayed for, when he prayed before His crucifixion. Intimacy with each other is accomplished by experiencing intimacy with God first.

Let's examine what true love looks like between Lovers. Once you know what it looks like, you'll be able to recognize it when it comes to you.

The Lovers' Secret Sauce: Harmonizing Vulnerability

Have you ever sung in public? How about sung a *solo* in public? Or how about sitting too close to your neighbor at church when the worship service starts? I grew up singing solos in church as a kid and progressed through school choirs, musicals, college coffee houses, and church worship teams. Last summer, twenty-some friends gathered around a campfire and asked for a song. I'd let music take a back seat for a number of years—like the back seat in a really long bus.

When I picked up the guitar and sang my first note, I instantly felt naked. Exposed. Vulnerable. After making it through the first verse, I felt myself enjoying it so much I didn't want the song to end. Then my daughter, eleven at the time, started to sing one of hers. The image of singing around the campfire seems so great until you're the one singing, and fear's grip can strangle. She faltered. The fireside audience went still, wondering if she could recover. I found the harmony in my head and ever so quietly, cautiously, blended my voice with hers until she absolutely flew. Her voice lifted, like the sparks on that fire, and left the whole group mesmerized and speechless. This is the beauty of harmonized vulnerability.

Harmonized vulnerability is a unique characteristic in close relationships where two people are safe, free, and encouraged to share weakness, insecurities, and their inner reality. The harmonizing occurs when the listener reflects to the speaker a sense of understanding and acceptance. When you listen to great music with harmony, you'll notice that the harmony cannot overpower or lead the melody; it must only complement. When my daughter faltered, it would have been a humiliating mistake for me to take over. But to add a quiet *harmony* to her exposed voice lifted her confidence to an angelic height.

Here is an example of a couple who sing a beautiful song of intimacy:

Pat and Harold

Pat: You know, you really hurt me tonight, Harold.

Harold: What? Is that what you're upset about? What did I do?

Pat: When you made that comment about me being "directionally challenged" and how I could get lost in my own neighborhood. And then all the men started laughing. That was so low.

Harold: Oh, you know that was only a joke. I didn't intend to hurt you. The guys knew it was a joke.

Pat: I don't care! Just because it was a joke doesn't make it okay. It was embarrassing!

Harold: Well, I'm sorry. I didn't mean to embarrass you.

Both Harold and Pat are silent. Pat could let it go at this, pour herself a glass of wine, and go to bed. But she decides to share more deeply.

Pat: You know, my dad used to ridicule my mom in front of other people. I would watch my mom laugh it off, but I knew she was shriveling inside. She became smaller and smaller and she's barely even there now. You know how she is.

Harold: I know.

Pat: I hate it when I feel I'm at the butt of someone else's joke. I know you never treat me like my dad treated my mom. But it hurts me deeply when you say things that embarrass me in front of other people.

Harold: I'm sorry, sweetie. I don't want to make you feel that way. Your dad was a real *$&@ to your mom. You know that's not me.

Pat: I know. I wish I wasn't so sensitive about it. But here I am, 55 years old, and it still gets to me. I'll try to give you the benefit of the doubt and let it go more easily. You promise to respect my need for privacy around your friends?

Harold: Of course. I already do, but I will do better about thinking before I speak.

Because Lovers practice effective communication, problem solving, and mutual encouragement, they have learned the other has their best interests in mind. Both have the power to deeply injure the other, and many times they do. But because they know how to empathize with the other's pain, they are quick to recognize their wounding behaviors and make efforts to stop. This isn't nirvana. It's just two people who've let go of their defenses, are willing to enter into their partner's pain and struggle, and come out stronger for it.

Intimacy

Humans naturally resist emotional intimacy. It's scary. It requires us to show up, to expose our deepest fears, to present our insecurities, and not fall apart in the process. It's like taking a sock and turning it inside out to expose the seam and sock lint. Or taking a pretty cross-stitched picture and looking at the back. Or taking your child's just-cleaned bedroom and looking under the bed where all the mess is hiding. We display the pretty side to the public, and we hide the inner workings because we judge them unpresentable for public display and unacceptable for human consumption.

Sheri and Luke's Story

Sheri slowly made her way to the kitchen where her husband Luke was drinking his coffee. She handed him the bottle of pain relievers and said with a wince, "How much am I supposed to take? I can't find the dosage."

Luke said, "I always take two."

"I know what *you* take, but I'm not you! Just tell me what the dosage says." Luke felt the cold edge in her voice.

Sheri was in obvious pain, but her curtness messaged Luke to "Keep clear!" and so he did. He read her the label and handed her the proper dosage. Sheri said thanks and left the kitchen.

Once she got back in bed, the spasms in her back screamed back at her with every shallow breath. Luke shouted, "Hope you feel better." Sheri heard the front door shut and then the silence of an empty house.

Sheri cried, partly because of the intense pain and partly because she needed tender loving care (TLC) from Luke, and she wasn't going to get it. She hated that she wanted TLC—it made her feel needy. Once the pain began to numb and the spasms quieted to a dull ache, she called Luke's cell phone.

"Sorry I snapped at you this morning about the dosage thing."

"Sorry I didn't help you more."

"I really wanted you to see the pain I was in and do something caring."

"Yeah, but you didn't tell me that. You didn't tell me the pain was worse, or what you needed, you just snapped at me."

"I know." Sheri paused and closed her eyes, readying herself to say the hard stuff. "I feel vulnerable when I have this much pain. I feel needy. I'm afraid you will judge me for being weak, or 'milking it,' so I try to just stay self-reliant. Then I end up sad that you don't care—like you abandon me when I need you most." Sheri choked out these words, fighting every self-protective impulse to keep them in. Exposing her true feelings felt so risky.

"But I do care," Luke said quietly. "You just need to tell me what you need. I don't want to make it worse, or make you feel needier. Just tell me what you need…without snapping at me."

"You're right. I will next time." Sheri felt the burden of guilt go and a familiar humble feeling take its place. She tries to apologize quicker these days. It beats the alternative of pointing fingers and standoffs.

"I don't think you're weak. I think you're strong, the strongest person I know."

"Thanks, hon. That means a lot," Sheri sighed in relief, and the pain in her back seemed remote and temporary. She really needed to hear him say that.

"Now is there anything you need when I get home from work? Something I can pick up at the store, or a massage maybe?"

Even though she knew it sounded cheesy, Sheri said, "Just you; you're all I need."

Luke smiled to himself. He kind of liked cheesy.

LULA Step 1: Don't keep wearing a Sock with a Rock

Sheri decided not to "overlook" or "forget about" the tiff. Maybe in the past, she would have avoided the conflict and just let the feelings fester. But this time, she decided to address it by calling Luke.

LULA Step 2: The Peace Offering

Out of the gate, Sheri offered an apology for her contribution to the conflict. Luke offered one of his own. Now they are two feet closer than they were before. They may have been on opposite sides of the tiff, but they were closer than before.

LULA Step 3: Exposing Sock Lint

Sheri assessed Luke's apology as a peace offering and sign of emotional safety, so she began to turn her soul-sock inside out for him to see. Without finger-pointing, blaming, or attacking, she told him what she wanted—for him to show that he cared about her pain.

LULA Step 4: Smelling the Dirty Sock, but Staying Put

Luke held his own. He didn't like being snapped at, and so he said so. But he appreciated not being blamed or attacked, so he stayed solid and open. He cared immensely about Sheri, and it bothered him that she still questioned it. That sock smells, but love keeps him there until it's resolved.

LULA Step 5: The Vulnerability Shake Out

Sheri went deeper into the sock and found the real problem—the rock that's been irritating her for years. But to get to the rock, she needs to expose all the innards of the dirty sock—the seam, the threads, the odor, the lint—you know, the stuff we like to keep hidden. That's when Sheri shares her *deepest* fears of being judged as weak and needy. She doesn't share these as *excuses* for snapping at Luke; she shares these as a bridge to emotional intimacy.

When Sheri was a child, being sick was unacceptable. No one went to the doctor. No one needed time off from work or school. If you were sick or injured, it was because you did something wrong, irresponsible, or silly. You could have and should have prevented it. It was better to just power through than to be sick. As an adult, Sheri found that these childhood expectations aren't effective, healthy, or wise. She wanted something different for herself. Sheri was given an opportunity to fill these old Soul Holes in the context of her Lovers Quadrant relationship with Luke. I'm proud of her for taking her healing seriously, aren't you?

In the Vulnerability Shake Out, Sheri tells what she is *ashamed of* (being weak) and what she is *afraid of* (being judged) and the resulting feelings (abandoned and sad). Luke's response is KEY! He's a rock star here, because instead of saying, "Those feelings and fears are dumb," he goes right into the stinky sock to fetch that rock. He speaks to the fear and shame by saying, "I don't think you're weak. I think you're strong—the strongest person I know."

LULA Step 6: Sock Transformation

In an instant, the sock is cleaned up, irritant-free, and double-infused with some pink fuzzy soft stuff. Sheri can sigh in relief because Luke filled her Soul Hole. Sheri could be stubborn and refuse his kind words as biased, but she doesn't. She receives them and lets the authentic, good, no-strings attached kind of love come on in.

She is *seen* as valuable and separate with unique needs and wants. She is *known* deeply with intimate understanding. And she is *accepted* unconditionally with authentic love. Presto! Finissimo! Fantastico! That's the good stuff, folks.

Sheri needed to be seen, known, and accepted by Luke for their relationship to move through the deadlock. Sheri needed to be vulnerable and share what was really going on with her, while Luke harmonized with that vulnerability with self-respect and love for

Sheri. Their story is one small example of what love looks like in the Lovers Quadrant.

"Most people are slow to champion love because they fear the transformation it brings into their lives. And make no mistake about it: love does take over and transform the schemes and operations of our egos in a very mighty way."

—*Aberjhani*

Qualities and Characteristics of LOVERS

You can recognize a tree by the type of fruit it produces. In an interview with Oprah, Maya Angelou taught something similar: "When someone shows you who they are, believe them."[49] People are not complete mysteries. You can learn a lot by observing them, if you know the qualities to look for. In recognizing Lovers, here are some tips:

Lovers are:

- **Morally motivated.** They do the right things for the right reasons. They don't do good things just to be recognized, admired, or to gain something. They do good things because it's the right thing to do.
- **Humble.** Lovers know how to eat crow, say they are sorry, admit wrongdoing, and own their contributions to a problem without shifting blame and pointing fingers.
- **Believers in equality.** Lovers believe each partner in the relationship has equal status, responsibility, position, and value. Both submit to one another in love.
- **Forgivers.** Lovers know how to forgive themselves for mistakes and failures, and they know how to forgive other people

---

49 http://www.oprah.com/omagazine/Oprah-Interviews-Maya-Angelou/7

too. Instead of holding on to regrets, they accept themselves as humans who are prone to error. Instead of holding grudges, they forgive others of their shortcomings and move on.

- **Self-respecters**. Lovers have self-respect. Having a healthy sense of self means they realize they are not more or less than who they are—an imperfect, worthwhile human. They know their strengths, weaknesses, desires, and needs, and they operate from self-acceptance. Because they respect themselves and their limits, they can respect others and their limits.

- **Self-aware**. They can identify their own feelings, needs, and motivations. They not only practice self-reflection, they also listen to feedback from others. They synthesize both into a healthy self-awareness.

- **Present.** Lovers know how to prioritize their attention so they can be fully present for themselves and the people who are important to them. Being present means focusing on the person or task at hand so intently that everything else takes a back seat.

- **Trustworthy.** They follow through, to the best of their ability, with what they say. They don't consistently say one thing and then do another.

- **Congruent.** What they say about themselves is consistent with their behavior. They don't hedge or parse their words as if they have something to hide. Body language, behavior, and their words are congruent, transparent, and honest.

A Few More Things Lovers Do

Lovers:

- Use collaboration instead of competition to solve problems.
- Are self-reflective and honest about their feelings.

- Avoid withdrawing, stonewalling, and passive aggression during conflict.
- Are assertive about their needs and wants, using direct communication.
- Listen reflectively when you have a problem without defensiveness.
- Operate with a low level of shame.
- Don't judge you or others with excessive criticism.
- View themselves as valuable and worthwhile, with a good measure of humility.
- Value accountability and companionship with honest, healthy people.
- Commit to personal growth and improvement.
- Stay in the Adult Functioning Mode during conflict. (They avoid adolescent tactics like name-calling, sarcasm, profanity, generalizations, and shouting.)
- Don't try to control you, your behaviors, or your emotions.
- Support your dreams and desires without neglecting their own.
- Accept you as the perfectly imperfect, growing, valuable person you are.
- Enjoy doing activities, sharing experiences, and being with you.
- Prioritize quality and quantity time together with you.
- Able to empathize with your feelings without fixing, controlling, or shutting down.

How it Feels to be in Relationship with a Lover

People in loving relationships experience a strong level of safety and security. They trust their partner completely and rarely worry about their commitment level, their honesty, or their integrity. They know that they are number one in their partner's life, and they rarely question their love. Over time, they have learned that, although challenges, stressors, and bad habits come and go, their partner's love and commitment is unchanging. They feel cared for, prioritized, and often admired, respected, and cherished. Each feels a profound sense of confidence derived from their shared love. This safety, unique to committed intimate relationships, allows them the freedom to explore parts of themselves without judgement, gives them room to be human without expectations of perfection, and offers fertile soil so they can bloom into their beautiful selves.

Lovers aren't perfect. They're learners.

Lovers are far from perfect; however, they are learners. They learn from their mistakes, their partners, and their ineffective patterns. They are people like you who read books like this. *They are willing to go to any length of self-discovery and vulnerability to achieve true intimacy with their partner.* Although exposure and vulnerability are scary, and feel like weakness, Lovers are willing to risk their ego for true intimacy. They are willing to look foolish, sound weak, and feel inadequate if it means deeper intimacy with their partner. They are true heroes of love.

Steps to Living in the Pink

R Restore order through boundaries

Often we find it difficult, if not impossible, to stand our ground, set a boundary, and follow through, especially with people we see as stronger than ourselves. Let's look at what boundaries are and why they are important.

Boundaries are invisible lines between you and someone else. Boundaries help you know where you end and where someone else begins. Boundaries allow you to protect what is valuable to you, and encourage you to be responsible for yourself, and for others to do the same. It has been said that strong fences make good neighbors, because once the neighbors know where the property line is, they can respect each other's space.

The bible says, "Above all else, guard your heart, for it is the wellspring of life."[50] The word *guard* here is also used when the bible speaks of guarding a prison. This type of guarding involves layers of security: barbed wire, men with guns, and heavy steel doors. Not just anything can get in and not just anything can get out without passing certain security criteria. That's how the bible talks about our heart. There is some precious stuff in the heart—life, love, joy, creativity, desire, holiness, and inspiration. It's a travesty to let an unworthy person or thing into the sacred place to wreak havoc or use it for selfish purposes.

When the fences are broken around your heart, any ole' person can saunter right in and take what he wants. Maybe that has happened to you. Your walls have been weakened, your fences blown down, your doors ripped off, and now the wellspring of your life is almost

50 Prv 4:23 (New International Version).

completely syphoned off. I'm sorry that's where you find yourself. It's a terrible place to be. You feel used up, flattened, and forgotten.

You may think you are hopeless, except for one little fact: you still have your heart. It's not gone. It may be bruised, battered, and sorely in need of protection, but it's still there. You may be afraid to set boundaries or to say "no." You've let things go so far for so long, it seems too late. Maybe you are afraid of what will happen if you do set a boundary with your partner. Maybe deep down, you believe if you set a boundary he will reject you, abandon you, or his anger will crush you. That fear has kept you from being authentic and whole for a long time. It's as if your partner is a filter that all things must pass through first. Before any little thing, you ask yourself what he will think or say before you buy something, read something, say something, or go somewhere. You are trying to protect yourself and your relationship by being pleasing to your partner. (Some women will do this for a strong-willed child/teen too.) Boundaries for you seem out of the question because you believe any boundary you set won't work.

The truth is, you *don't* know how your partner will respond to your boundaries. You don't know if you'll get the cold shoulder, an angry outburst, or dismissed altogether. One thing you do know is if you do nothing, you'll get the same ol' same ol'. Consider taking a step of faith toward healthy self-care. Nothing will change if *you* don't change things yourself.

Respecting one another's boundaries is still of supreme importance, even for the couple who has been married a long time. Personality differences become even more glaring with enough time and history. These personality differences are complementary to one another, how an introvert complements an extrovert, or a numbers person complements a creative type. However, these personality differences can also be a source of great frustration. Each partner should be aware of the temptation to change, control, or judge their partner's personality to fit their own. This is a violation of healthy boundaries. Each partner should have the freedom to express their personality differences in the context of love and respect.

Respecting one another's boundaries is an ongoing challenge in every relationship. Here is an exercise to help you along the way:

- Write down three things you believe <u>your partner values about his/her own personality</u>. Example: "I believe my husband values his ability to be disciplined in the areas of work and exercise. I believe my husband values and is proud of his love and proficiency for golf. I also think that my husband values how close he is with his extended family (i.e., his mom and dad)."

- Now list three things <u>YOU value about your partner's personality</u>. Example: "I really appreciate the way my husband puts the kids first, above other things like work or golf. I like how he prioritizes them. I also value my husband's attention to his self-care by working out. I also value my husband's nurturing personality; it feels good to have him care for me when I need it."

- Now write down three things <u>you value about YOUR own personality</u>. Example: "I value my drive for social interaction and social planning. I value the courage I have to try new things. I also like the tenacity and endurance I have shown by going back to school for my degree."

- Now compare the lists and see what they have in common. This is a good way to not only validate each other's personality and character, but also to compare your priorities without judgement. You will have the opportunity to step into the other person's shoes and see yourself from their perspective. Take a moment to talk about these differences. Instead of judging his love for golf or voracious work habits, acknowledge his priorities and personality as different and valuable.

- Make a commitment to one another to value and appreciate your differences and to purposely see them as complements to your own personality. Instead of seeing yourselves as opposing competitive forces, see yourselves as a team with each member having different strengths. Commit to stop trying to change one another and instead, accept each other as-is.

E Experience God

Lovers realize that only God can fill the God-sized hole in their lives, and looking to your partner to fill that hole only results in frustration. Lovers know that their partners are unable to provide 100% of what is needed 100% of the time. Lovers know that their partners will disappoint them from time to time. However, a Lover's overarching goal is to see, know, and love, even if they're offered imperfectly.

Lovers prioritize their relationship with God above their relationship with their partner. They realize that they first receive God-sized love from God, enabling them to feel Seen, Known, and Unconditionally Accepted. Out of this fountain of God-energized affection, they are able and willing to give to their partner without fear of rejection.

One way to deepen intimacy with your partner is to pray out loud together. Praying out loud together is often an emotionally binding experience between two people because of prayer's private nature. Praying together is important because it moves the couple into deeper vulnerability. When you are vulnerable with each other, sharing your fears and weaknesses, your understanding and compassion for one another increases.

If you are unfamiliar with praying out loud together, try something like this:

"God, thank you for giving us each other and helping us love better. We are sorry for hurting one another sometimes. Help us to catch ourselves earlier, before we say hurtful things. We want to love each other the way you love us. Amen."

Prayer is unique among all therapeutic exercises because of the way it disarms our defenses. During prayer, we do things that don't come naturally, like ask for help. We say things during prayer we don't usually say anywhere else, like admit our wrongs. That's why praying together can initially feel uncomfortable, especially if we are not used to being that open with one another. However, prayer is an important way for couples to become united and strong enough to face their challenges together.

If your partner doesn't want to pray out loud, ask if it would be okay if he/she prays with you while you pray out loud. Remember that respecting one another's boundaries is paramount, and if one partner feels too uncomfortable, coerced, or pushed, then that's not a loving gesture.

Some Christian circles encourage the man to be the Spiritual Leader of the woman in marriage. Common Christian thought instructs a husband to lead in all things Christian: prayer, bible study, churchgoing, tithing, and child rearing. There are inherent dangers in this view:

1. Men feel overly pressured to meet the vague and unwritten expectations of the Spiritual Leader role, resulting in husbands' feelings of failure and wives' feelings of disappointment.

2. Women feel less power to express needs or concerns because of their perceived inequality and/or hierarchy of the marriage.

3. Women may confront problems less assertively and set fewer needed boundaries for themselves and their children when they feel they have lesser responsibility.

4. The bible never specifically instructs husbands to be the spiritual leaders of their wives. (See Ephesians 5:21-33)

5 If a woman feels she should submit to her husband spiritually, she has effectively replaced God's authority with her husband's—listening to her husband is equal to listening to God. She puts her husband in between herself and God. This is devastating to a woman's sense of autonomy, privacy, personal power, and spiritual health.

6. Many times, the woman is the spiritually motivated spouse, emphasizing church, prayer, and religious activities. Valuing faith and spiritual connection is a gift and a blessing, and doesn't need to be minimized if her spouse does not share the same motivation.

I've found the marriages that work the best are ones in which each person can express his/her natural and spiritual gifts with freedom and appropriateness, where each other's differences and strengths are accepted and respected, and when both share responsibilities out of mutual submission.

Experiencing God is both a personal and shared practice. Experiencing God is for everyone who wants it. Experiencing God surpasses rank, hierarchies, class systems, and gender, and can happen anywhere at any time. Making a practice of experiencing God is paramount for the Lover because she knows her relationship with God is the only thing truly keeping her together. The Lover realizes in his depths that without the work of God in his life, he would be lost and alone. Lovers grasp that their most unifying factor is the love of God that surpasses what either of them can do on their own.

P Provide yourself with people

- **Friends:** Lovers know that their partner cannot fulfill all their social and intellectual needs, and that friends are essential. Lovers know the value that friends, support groups, and community give to their partners. Lovers know the importance of sharing their partner with friends. Lovers encourage their partners to have other healthy relationships.

- **Small Groups:** From time to time, Mr. Dashing and I facilitate a couples' small group from our church. It's usually pretty combustible with hot food, rowdy kids, and stimulating conversation. We talk about work and kids and marriage and the Seahawks. We talk about the sermon that week at church and how God makes a difference in our lives. Some of us drink wine, some of us don't. Some of us pray out loud, some of us don't. Some of us bring our bibles, some of us don't. But all of us give the gift of friendship and support to one another. I think it's what Jesus prayed for the night before he laid down his life to save us. I'm happy that our little group is an answer to His prayer.

- **Counseling:** Lovers also know the importance of asking for professional help as needed. They realize that they don't have all the answers and all the skills to make a marriage work for a lifetime. They understand that they can't see what they can't see. They understand the value of paying a professional to give an unbiased perspective of their unique relationship dynamics and patterns. Lovers in healthy relationships often will keep a therapist "on tap" for times they can't work something out. Establishing a working relationship with a marriage counselor is one of the smartest things Lovers in relationships do. They know that going to counseling is like regular exercise, just like eating your brussels sprouts, or getting your teeth cleaned. It's just part of the deal. Mr. Dashing and I both go to a counselor as needed. It would be silly not to.

S Seek Intimacy

Lovers realize their relationship is never as good as it gets. There is always deeper, always stronger, always lovelier. The human soul is a map for exploration, with lands that are still untouched and pristine. The couple who goes deeper and reaches further will never be disappointed by the gems they find within the heart of their partner.

Intimacy is marked by familiarity, a warm friendship developing through long association, suggesting informal warmth or privacy.[51] It takes effort, time, and trust. It doesn't come easy because we treat intimacy like a dental visit—we resist it, and put it off, and make up excuses to avoid it. We like walls, doors, and locks. Opening ourselves up to intimacy incurs risk, invites judgment, and leaves us unprotected. It's not comfortable. We feel exposed, raw, and needy. We tell ourselves, "If I invite someone to know me intimately, they will find out who I really am, and they'll reject me for sure!" But seeking intimacy is absolutely necessary to strengthen yourself and your relationships. You simply can't have the depth, love, and joy in a relationship without it. Let's take a snapshot of what intimacy is and isn't.

---

51 *Merriam-Webster's Collegiate Dictionary,* Eleventh ed., s.v. "intimacy."

Intimacy is not:

- Nagging your partner to open up or express his feelings
- Intensity of feelings
- Just sexual in nature

Intimacy is:

- Knowing and expressing your feelings in non-accusatory language
- Sharing weaknesses, fears, and vulnerabilities without fear of judgment or control
- Validating your partner's experiences and feelings without judging, controlling, or taking them personally

NEEDS and INTIMACY Exercise

1. One partner should list and prioritize five specific needs he/she has. For example, *"1. Treat me like an equal with the words you use. 2. Help me discipline the children. 3. Go to church with me. 4. Come home for dinner each night at a reasonable time or call me when you'll be late. 5. Go with me for walks at night once the kids are fed."*

2. This partner shares her list in full while the other listens without speaking.

3. The other partner should list and prioritize five specific needs he/she has. For example, *"1. I want you to stop criticizing me in public. 2. I need less complaining from you and more appreciation. 3. I don't just want obligatory sex; I want you to actually want to have sex with me. 4. I'd like more date nights for just the two of us. 5. I need to feel loved and wanted by you."*

4. Now this partner shares his list in full while the other listens without speaking.

5. Each person must acknowledge the other's list with respect and understanding. Instead of criticizing the other person's needs, talk about ways that you both can work as a team to make these requests possible.

6. Now, note how you feel once you have stated your needs and problem-solved together. The idea is to work toward intimacy in a safe atmosphere of sharing and acceptance. Each of you can take ownership of ways you can connect with your partner in ways that he/she values.

7. If you don't see eye to eye on one or two items, then work on the ones you both feel good about, and table the other items for a counseling session or until a later time. You don't have to have all five nailed down perfectly to reap the benefits of better intimacy.

Repair Work

Lovers have a toolbox of skills for conflict resolution and problem solving. That doesn't mean they solve everything easily or right away, but it does mean they know how to use communication skillfully to get closer instead of farther away. Here is an exercise that slows down the conflict spiral effect and helps Lover couples negotiate difficult conversations:

ABCs of Conflict Resolution

Difficult situations, differences of opinions, and painful challenges have the power to derail intimacy, but not if they're navigated with skill. The ABCs of Conflict Resolution will help you do just that.

It is simply the following formula: *"When you do or say A, I feel B. I want you to do C instead so I can feel close to you."*

The ABCs of Conflict Resolution guides a couple away from attacking and blaming and toward the heart of the issue. Using "I feel" language aids the speaker in owning his/her own emotions without using attacking language. Here is an example:

George and Anne have been married six years and have a three-year-old daughter. Each feels uncared for and unloved in their marriage since their daughter was born. They don't want to divorce but know they need to rekindle their love for one another now before it gets worse. George starts out.

ABCs of Conflict Resolution: George's Turn

STEP 1: George tells Anne how he feels with "I" language, being careful not to use accusatory language: "I feel rejected when you say 'no' to sex. It's okay once in a while. I understand that you're tired and that our daughter takes a lot of your energy. But I want to be close to you, and when you turn me down, I start to feel distant and sometimes even angry. I feel like I'm the least important thing in your life."

STEP 2: Anne listens reflectively and paraphrases back to George what she heard without interjecting her own defenses or excuses. "I heard you say that you feel rejected and not important when I turn you down for sex. You said that you know that I'm tired, but that you feel bad and angry when I say 'no.' Did I hear you right?"

STEP 3: Checking for understanding is an important step because it gives the speaker the chance to feel heard. Once Anne checks for clarity, then George has an opportunity to respond. George says, "Yes, that's right. I want you to know how it makes me feel when you turn me down. It feels bad."

STEP 4: Empathize, empathize, empathize. This is Anne's opportunity to draw close to George and step into his shoes for a second.

This is where the magic is, where intimacy can really blossom. Anne says, "I get it. I know what it feels like to be rejected, and I get it. It feels terrible. I'm sorry. I'm sorry that you feel that way, and that you feel rejected by me. The last thing I want to make you feel is unimportant to me. Because you are. You are important to me."

STEP 5: Now it's time for George to follow up with his request. "I understand that sometimes you'll be too tired, but I want you to say 'yes' more often. I want you to WANT to make love. I want you to WANT me." Whoa, George just got REAL! George became the most vulnerable he has ever been with Anne. This kind of statement takes a lot of courage to say out loud, so Anne shouldn't miss this opportunity to show love and care.

STEP 6: Anne's response and commitment to action: "Okay, I understand. You need to feel wanted by me. You need to feel desired. I'm in. I will make an effort to reserve some time just for us. I'll make an effort to put you before other things that can wait."

Wow, did that seem too easy? Are you thinking, "Yeah, but … that's not going to work with us…" The key to the ABCs of Conflict Resolution is that both parties resist the temptation to be defensive, critical, sarcastic, accusatory, or avoidant. Both partners must agree to these rules, or the ABCs will not work, and the couple will stay stuck in perpetual conflict over the same issue, year after year after year. Would you like to see Anne try it? Okay, let's see how she does.

ABCs of Conflict Resolution: Anne's Turn

STEP 1: Anne tells George how she feels with "I" language, being careful not to use accusatory or critical words. "I feel overly responsible for you when you ask me for sex. It's like I don't get to just rest after a long day. I work, come home, take care of our baby, clean up, and all I want to do is just relax. But when you want sex, I feel like

I have to take care of you too. And I just don't want to! I'm tired of taking care of everyone else but me."

STEP 2: George listens reflectively to Anne's complaint and paraphrases back to her what he heard without interjecting his own thoughts or defenses. "Okay, you feel overly responsible to take care of me and my desire for sex. You just want to relax, but you feel like you're responsible to take care of me. Is that right?"

STEP 3: George checks for understanding so that Anne can feel heard. "Yes, totally responsible for making you happy. And then I feel pressured, and you seem totally needy. And then I'm not even attracted to you because you seem like a chore that needs to be done. I just can't do it all. I feel overwhelmed by all the expectations!"

STEP 2 AGAIN: Anne has a lot to say, so George is going to return to STEP 2 and 3: "All right, you feel like sex is a chore, that you feel pressure from too many expectations, and that I'm needy. Is that right?" George is staying present here and not letting her words make him angry. Anne's words may sting, but he must stay present in this moment without getting defensive or angry.

STEP 3 AGAIN: Anne says, "Yes, that's basically it."

STEP 4: Empathize, empathize, empathize. This is George's opportunity to draw closer to Anne and put himself in her shoes. He needs to be careful to avoid building defenses or giving excuses, and just empathize. "I understand. I know how it feels to never 'clock out,' or never get a break. I know how it feels to be needed all the time when there's no time just for you. I'm sorry that some of my persistence has made you feel like sex is a chore. I'm not needy. I'm not a sex fiend. I don't *need* anything from you."

STEP 5: Now it's time for Anne to follow up with her request. "Thank you. I appreciate that. I don't know how to fix this. But I have a few ideas…"

Anne and George brainstorm ideas to make their new situation work. They think about scheduling a date night that George would plan so that Anne wouldn't feel responsible. They think about George putting their baby down before Anne gets home from work, so she and he can have time together instead of her feeling like she has to put the baby down before she can rest.

STEP 6: George's response and commitment to action: "I will put the baby down before you get home from work on Wednesdays. I'll have some food put together so when you get home, we can just sit, eat, and relax."

Anne replies, "I think that will really help. And I promise that at least on those nights, I will reserve my heart, thoughts, and energy for intimacy with you. I promise to genuinely want to do it. I won't just go through the motions."

George and Anne successfully worked through an ongoing conflict that both were struggling with for months. Each had felt neglected and alone. They may have been tempted to blame the other for their feelings, and defend themselves as being "right," but that would only have forced them further apart. Instead, they moved closer together, finding a solution that made them feel heard and cared for. Their emotional and sexual intimacy improved at all levels.

Fair Fighting Rules

Conflicts, hurt feelings, and differing viewpoints are all things couples fight over. Every couple fights, but only Lovers know how to fight fair. Fighting fair is a way to air a grievance or communicate a complaint so Lovers can get back to doing what they do best—loving. Fighting fair makes it okay to communicate your needs and goals while hearing the needs and goals of your partner. Lovers have learned how to do this without turning their fights into World War III. Here are some Fighting Don'ts and Fighting Do's for deeper intimacy.

Fighting Don'ts

1. Don't be defensive.
2. Don't use sarcasm.
3. Don't use profanity.
4. Don't call each other names.
5. Don't use generalizations (always and never).
6. Don't walk away angry.
7. Don't judge the other's motives.
8. Don't punish with silence.
9. Don't scream.
10. Don't get physical (including slamming doors, throwing things, grabbing, pushing, or hitting.)

When couples start breaking the fair fighting rules, the fight escalates and damage is done that takes months to heal. Games, sports, and debate matches have rules to keep the players playing fair. But when fighting couples put anger and pain in charge of the rules, both sides end up losing.

Fear of abandonment and being controlled compel couples to dig their heels in on their side of the issue. They gather facts and fictions to build a case against their partner, which creates more distance between the couple. Each couple has the capacity to draw closer together, to collaborate to solve problems, and to share each other's burdens and joys. Only the Lovers choose the greater path toward Intimacy.

Fighting Do's:

1. Do express your concerns, needs, and goals.
2. Do directly communicate what you want.
3. Do share your feelings.
4. Do listen reflectively.
5. Do stay calm.
6. Do take a ten-minute break if the argument gets too heated and then come back to the discussion.
7. Do own your part and apologize as necessary.
8. Do offer forgiveness.
9. Do stay with it—you're almost there.
10. Do reach out to touch, hug, and kiss after a fight.

The LULA Way: Lovers realize that conflict is not only an unavoidable part of life together, but that conflict is an opportunity to draw closer than they were before the conflict arose. They see problems as things to overcome, not fear. They embrace differences of opinion as things that sharpen them, not defeat them. Lovers believe the truth about being one flesh in God, even if they don't feel it or see it sometimes. Lovers push past their fears of abandonment and control and intimacy because the reward is greater than the risk. Lovers are true champions of the good news of what Jesus prayed: "May they be brought to complete unity to let the world know that you sent me and have loved them even as you have loved me."[52] Lovers are not afraid to reach out and draw close even when their pride resists intimacy. Lovers are the bravest people I know.

---

53 Jn 17:23 (New International Version).

Chapter 8

Your New Life the LULA Way

"The most beautiful people we have known are those who have known defeat, known suffering, known struggle, known loss, and have found their way out of the depths. These persons have an appreciation, a sensitivity, and an understanding of life that fills them with compassion, gentleness, and a deep loving concern. Beautiful people do not just happen."

—Elisabeth Kübler-Ross

"Since the beginning, our road has not been easy. Our experience as missionaries in South America was very difficult. We home-schooled three kids, sent two to college, and one to rehab. We've dealt with Johnathan being laid off and out of work. We've weathered my chronic depression and his same sex attractions. We've taken care of our daughter's kids while she went to drug rehab. We've been through a lot. And we've been through it together." Angela looked over at Johnathan, and he put his hand on her knee.

There was something about this couple that made me flounder. They were sitting in my office for their third session, wanting me to help them sort through some issues, and I felt like the tables should really be turned. I felt like I should be the one coming to them for the secret to their success.

Angela and Johnathan had been married forty-six years, and had seen countries, children, jobs, and sickness come and go before their eyes. They came to counseling together to address her depression and his response to it. I felt like a novice sitting there in front of them, even though I had been in practice for over 15 years. I was pretty sure that whatever I helped them accomplish, I was going to get the better end of the deal, gleaning from the years of wisdom collected between them.

Though Angela and Johnathan had overcome many obstacles together, they felt like there were still some things they needed to do to be happy in their upcoming retirement years. I started asking some questions about Angela's childhood and when her depression started. Her father was a minister and left most of the parenting to his wife. He took special care to take her younger brothers fishing and to coach their sports, but took little interest in Angela. She rarely felt pretty, or important, or even worthy of notice in her traditional, conservative Presbyterian home. Angela reported that for much of her childhood, she felt invisible. From an early age, she remembers asking why God made her.

When I asked her what triggered her recent bout with depression, Angela was stumped. Finally, Johnathan interjected his opinion. "Angela, did you start feeling bad when I took on that group of young interns?"

Silence hung like a fog until Angela looked down and said, "I don't know." As Johnathan explained a bit more, I learned that a group of college-aged men were doing a stint in Johnathan's department and he was in charge of facilitating part of their program.

Angela admitted that at first his time and attention to their needs was okay with her, but then she started feeling jealous of the excitement he expressed while talking about them after work. Angela, instead of talking about this with him, withdrew into her past feelings of rejection. These feelings were so second nature to her, she barely recognized she was slipping into her dark hole. The more she withdrew, the more time Johnathan spent away from home.

Since Jonathan hadn't identified himself as gay, neither did I. Instead, I asked, "How have you managed to stay in your marriage while you're having same-sex attractions?"

"Well, like a lot of guys like me, I thought if I got married, the attractions would go away. When that wasn't the case, I told a pastor friend of mine about them. I've always loved Angela, and I knew I didn't want to leave her for anything, so he started helping me. I've been in accountability groups for 30 years."

"And you've never cheated? Never strayed? Never regretted your decision to marry?"

"No," Johnathan answered, looking downcast. I knew this conversation was hard for him. I knew he felt a sense of shame. I could tell that he had come to peace with himself, after many years of struggle, but that talking about it with someone new brought some of the pain back.

"How has this affected you, Angela?"

She reached over to take Johnathan's hand. "Sometimes I'm fine, and sometimes I'm not. I think Johnathan is right. When he showed interest in having the interns at the office, I felt second best." She let a tear fall.

"You guys have had this conversation before, haven't you?"

Johnathan answered, "Oh yes, many times. And no matter what, it still hurts."

"Why? Tell me about that."

"Well, she feels rejected, and I feel like she doesn't trust me. I'm powerless to change that part of myself, but I know it hurts her. I've never acted on my attractions, but I can't change them either."

"And you, Angela? How has it affected you?"

Angela looked up at him, and both shared a moment of understanding that only forty-six years together could bring. She said, "I hate that I'm not stronger, and more confident. I hate that I let it bother me. I know he is true to me. He always has been. But I'm afraid that I'll never be what he really wants. That I'll never be enough."

Johnathan said, "I feel the same way. I feel like I'll never be able to give her what she really needs. I'm sorry that I've hurt you with this, Angela. I wish I could change it, but I can't. I wish you didn't have to deal with this. But I made a decision a long time ago to be faithful to you. Now we have forty-six years together and kids and grandkids because of it. I don't regret that decision, but I do regret that you've felt this way."

After a few more questions, I learned that the mechanics of sex were working fine for them. Johnathan reported that although he was sexually attracted to men, and had been since he could remember, he could be sexually aroused by Angela too. Angela reported that she never felt like he *wasn't* sexually attracted to her, but that certain men were more enticing to him. She said that it wasn't easy to live with, but that they have coped with it for many years. She said that she supposed her depression wasn't easy to live with either, so they were even.

We sat for a while, letting the reality of their marriage sink in and the feelings take their place. I said to Johnathan, "I know you might feel put on the spot, but will you do something right now?"

Johnathan nodded. "Will you put your arm around Angela and let me guide you both through some imagery? You're going to go back in time and imagine having a conversation with Angela's dad, okay?"

They both closed their eyes and I painted a picture of them both going back to Angela's childhood. They pictured themselves holding hands while they saw the invisible-feeling child watching her excited father take her brothers fishing. They imagined watching them pull away from the house and then they imagined together how small Angela would be feeling left at the house. I asked them to imagine her face, her hair, her clothes, and the expression in her eyes. At this point in the exercise, Angela began to cry great, heaving sobs, and Johnathan's hand tightened on her shoulder.

"Now, Johnathan, tell little Angela what she desperately needs to hear right now."

Johnathan fumbled to find the words a bit, and then as if inspired, landed hard on this, "He should have taken you, Angela. If I were him, I would have taken you. I never would have left you at the house." Johnathan let hot tears roll down his face, and Angela nodded with eyes still closed. We let each image have the time it needed and then I asked them to do one more thing.

"Now, I want you to imagine Angela's dad coming home. The boys wash up for dinner, and Angela's dad parks the car in the garage. Johnathan, I want you to go in the garage, and I want you to talk to Angela's dad. I want you to tell him what he needs to hear."

We all breathed deeply as Johnathan prepared the image of what this conversation would sound like. Johnathan said, "You're missing out on a really pretty little girl. You're preoccupied with your boys, but you're missing out on Angela. And that's your loss." Johnathan's voice cracked. "You're her father, and you should pay attention to her. How sad that you are missing out on someone so precious." At this point, Johnathan couldn't go on. He opened his eyes and turned Angela's shoulders square to his. "That's true, Angela. That's true."

Angela hugged Johnathan so tight, I wasn't sure he could breathe. She whispered, "thank you" again and again, and he just held on until they sighed and released each other. At this point, I felt like I just won the Nobel Peace Prize. I felt like someone gave me an unexpected gift. How in the world did I get so lucky that God would make me part of this marvelous moment of shared love? I wiped at my eyes and told them that *I* should probably pay *them* for this session, and we laughed.

Johnathan, in all his humanity and feelings of shame, completely imperfect, reached back into Angela's past and redeemed her self-worth with her. Both revealed their profound sense of inadequacy to one another and felt love in return. This unconditional love drills down deep into the soul—it goes to where the pain is and heals it. Johnathan and Angela reached a new depth of intimacy and a new height of joy. Together.

In future sessions, Angela reported knowing deeply for the first time that Johnathan's same-sex attractions had nothing to do with her, and that she could accept him fully and unconditionally, just as he accepted her. Her depression began to lift, and she felt glad that Johnathan wanted to work on some Soul Holes from his past as well. Since much of Angela's self-doubt had dissipated, she reported enjoying sex more with Johnathan. To that, Johnathan said, "I always enjoy sex with Angela, because it's Angela." Angela smiled shyly, and the two of them felt more together and less afraid.

My work with Johnathan and Angela isn't a prescription for marriages facing similar struggles, but it is an accurate description of their experience, their feelings, and their story.

Each had their own Soul Holes to address. Life delivered many challenges for them to work through, but these two chose to turn their challenges into opportunities for greater intimacy. They didn't face their human temptations, imperfections, and fears alone. They did it together.

. . . .

They turned what could have been huge deal breakers into love-makers. This is what Lovers do.

. . . .

You have your own story, your own feelings, and your own experiences. You have your own set of unique challenges that are very different, yet very much the same as everyone else's. God knows. You have probably started the process of identifying and addressing your own Soul Holes. You may be working through them as we speak. You may look back at the times you felt forgotten or the object of someone's ridicule, and see your child self, like Angela did. Maybe you taste that old pain like it was yesterday. You see how those emotional wounds are the root cause of much of your unhappiness and relational distress.

They don't have to be anymore.

Now, you have the information and power to change your relationships from the inside out. You know now that the Vital Three must overwhelm you with their power, uproot you from your old patterns, and point you in a new direction. As you **see** yourself as valuable, you **know** yourself deeply, and you offer yourself **unconditional acceptance**, your Soul Holes will fill. The dysfunction that your Soul Holes caused in the past will be replaced with effective relational patterns. You will no longer be appealing to Losers, Users, or Abusers because you will have outgrown them. You, however, will be undeniably appealing to people on the same path of growth and healing. So, get ready to be irresistible to people who **see** you, **know** you, and **accept** you just the way you are. Get ready to experience authentic love. Get ready to embark on your new life.

Your relationships are lucky and blessed to have you, and you can make a difference in them!

Resources

National Domestic Violence Hotline
    1-800-799-SAFE
    1-800-799-7233

National Suicide Prevention Hotline
    1-800-273-TALK
    1-800-273-8255

Safe Helpline for the Military Community
    1-877-955-5247
    www.safehelpline.org

BOOKS

Lundy Bancroft, *Why Does He Do That? Inside the Minds of Angry and Controlling Men*

Pia Mellody. *The Intimacy Factor: The Ground Rules for Overcoming Obstacles to Truth, Respect and Lasting Love*

Leslie Vernick, *The Emotionally Destructive Marriage: How to Find Your Voice and Reclaim Your Hope*

Susan Weitzman, *Not to People like Us: Hidden Abuse in Upscale Marriages*

Henry Cloud and John Townsend, *Boundaries: When to Say Yes, and When to Say No to Take Control of Your Life*

Melody Beattie, *Journey to the Heart: Daily Meditations on the Path to Freeing Your Soul*

Bibliography

Bancroft, Lundy. *Why Does He Do That? Inside the Minds of Angry and Controlling Men.* Berkley Books, New York, NY. 2002.

Browne A, Finkelhor D: Impact of child sexual abuse: a review of the literature. *Psychological Bulletin* 1986;99:66–77 [PubMed].

Bureau of Justice. Bureau of Justice Statistics. *Homicide Trends from 1976-1999* (2001).

Capouya, Emile. *Classic English Love Poems.* New York: Hippocrene Books, 1998.

Carnes, Patrick J. *The Betrayal Bond: Breaking Free of Exploitive Relationships.* Health Communications, Inc. Dearfield Beach, Florida. 1997.

De Becker, Gavin. *The Gift of Fear: and Other Survival Signals That Protect Us from Violence.* New York: Dell Publishing, 1999.

Douglas, K. A. "Results From the 1995 National College Health Risk Behavior Survey." *Journal of American College Health* 46 (1997): 55-66.

Finkelhor, Turner, Ormrod, Hamby and Kracke. National Survey of Children's Exposure to Violence, OJJDP, *Juvenile Justice Bulletin* (October 2009).

Gottman, J and Neil Jacobson. *When Men Batter Women.* New York: Simon and Schuster, 1998.

Hotchkiss, Sandy. *Why is it Always about You? The Seven Deadly Sins of Narcissism.* Firepress, New York, NY. 2002.

Levy, Michael S., *A Helpful Way to Conceptualize and Understand Reenactments*, v. 7 (3) The Journal of Psychotherapy Practice and Research courtesy of American Psychiatric Publishing, 1998.

Mellody, Pia., Freundlich, Lawrence S. *The Intimacy Factor: The Ground Rules of Overcoming the Obstacles to Truth, Respect, and Lasting Love.* Harper Collins, New York, NY. 2003.

Peck, M. Scott. *People of the Lie: Hope for Healing Human Evil.* Touchstone, New York, NY. 1983.

Rink, Margaret J. *Can Christians Love Too Much? Breaking the Cycle of Codependency*, Grand Rapids: Zondervan, 1989.

Rink, Margaret J. *Christian Men Who Hate Women: Healing Hurting Relationships*, Grand Rapids: Zondervan, 1990.

Rosenberg, Ross. *The Human Magnet Syndrome: Why We Love People Who Hurt Us.* Eau Claire, WI: PESI Publishing and Media, 2013.

Russell DEH: *The Secret Trauma: Incest in the Lives of Girls and Women.* New York, Basic Books, 1986

Scott, Lisa E. *It's All About Him: How to Identify and Avoid the Narcissist Male Before You Get Hurt.* Springville, UT: Cedar Fort, Inc, 2009.

Simon, Jr., George, *In Sheep's Clothing: Understanding and Dealing with Manipulative People.* Parkhurst Brothers, United States of America. 2010.

van der Kolk BA, Greenberg MS: *The psychobiology of the trauma response: hyperarousal, constriction, and addiction to traumatic reexposure, in Psychological Trauma*, edited by van der Kolk BA. Washington, DC, American Psychiatric Press, 1987, 63–87.

Warshaw, Robin. *I Never Called It Rape*. New York:HarperCollins Publishers, 1994.

Dr. Jane McGregor and Tim McGregor, *The Empathy Trap: Understanding Antisocial Personalities* (London: Sheldon Press, 2013). Retrieved from http://www.sott.net/article/268449-Empathic-people-are-natural-targets-for-sociopaths-protect-yourself, 9/26/2014.

CPSIA information can be obtained
at www.ICGtesting.com
Printed in the USA
FSHW012306081118
53654FS